on track ...
Spirit

every album, every song

Rev. Keith A. Gordon

SONIC**BOND**

sonicbondpublishing.com

Sonicbond Publishing Limited
www.sonicbondpublishing.co.uk
Email: info@sonicbondpublishing.co.uk

First Published in the United Kingdom 2023
First Published in the United States 2023

British Library Cataloguing in Publication Data:
A Catalogue record for this book is available from the British Library

Copyright Keith A. Gordon 2023

ISBN 978-1-78952-248-8

Typeset in ITC Garamond & ITC Avant Garde
Printed and bound in England

Graphic design and typesetting: Full Moon Media

Acknowlegements

Thanks, as always, to Brother Willie Jemison, Steve Morley, Bill Claypool, Threk Michaels, Bill Glahn, Sharon Underwood, and, of course, my lovely wife Tracey.

Thanks are also due to Rick DiBello, who introduced me to Spirit as a teenager, launching a lifelong obsession with this wonderful band; to Stephen Lambe for allowing me to become part of the Sonicbond Publishing family; to Rick Johnson and Bill Knight, my first mentors in the world of rock criticism, and to friends, colleagues and collaborators like Cary Baker, Ira Robbins, Dave Marsh, Fred Mills, Martin Popoff, Bill Holdship, John Kordosh, Daryl Sanders, Jim Testa, Greg Prevost, Henry Yates, Ron Hart, Art Tipaldi and Lester Bangs - all of whom have aided and abetted my efforts through the years.

Special thanks to Mick Skidmore and the Randy C. Wolfe Trust for their help and support for this project, and to Bob Irwin and Jay Millar of Sundazed Records for the groovy pix!

Dedicated to Thom King and Len Rossi - two longtime friends, both of whom inspired and challenged me in numerous ways for decades.

Would you like to write for Sonicbond Publishing?
We are mainly a music publisher, but we also occasionally publish in other genres including film and television. At Sonicbond Publishing we are always on the look-out for authors, particularly for our two main series, On Track and Decades.

Mixing fact with in depth analysis, the On Track series examines the entire recorded work of a particular musical artist or group. All genres are considered from easy listening and jazz to 60s soul to 90s pop, via rock and metal.

The Decades series singles out a particular decade in an artist or group's history and focuses on that decade in more detail than may be allowed in the On Track series.

While professional writing experience would, of course, be an advantage, the most important qualification is to have real enthusiasm and knowledge of your subject. First-time authors are welcomed, but the ability to write well in English is essential.

Sonicbond Publishing has distribution throughout Europe and North America, and all our books are also published in E-book form. Authors will be paid a royalty based on sales of their book.
Further details about our books are available from
www.sonicbondpublishing.com. To contact us, complete the contact form there or email info@sonicbondpublishing.co.uk

on track ...

Spirit

Contents

Introduction: From Rising Sons to Spirits Rebellious

Even in the late-1960s era of innovation and freedom in rock music, Spirit stood head-and-shoulders above their contemporaries. Perhaps only Arthur Lee's Love shared the same expansive and adventurous artistic vision as the five guys in Spirit, whose disparate and diverse musical backgrounds led the band to explore the outer regions of rock 'n' roll, as the band incorporated elements of the blues, folk, R&B and jazz into their heady brew of psychedelia-tinted hard rock. Though they never experienced the level of commercial success that their talents and innovative music deserved, few bands since have matched Spirit in eccentricity, originality, intensity and instrumental virtuosity.

Spirit's roots can be traced back to 1965 and the then-up-and-coming Los Angeles blues rock outfit Rising Sons. Formed by 17-year-old multi-instrumentalist prodigy Ry Cooder, singer/guitarists Jesse Lee Kincaid and Taj Mahal, bassist Gary Marker and drummer Ed 'Cass' Cassidy, Rising Sons quickly made a name for themselves on the cutthroat L.A. music scene, performing at legendary venues like The Troubadour and The Ash Grove. The band signed with the prestigious Columbia Records, and recorded an album produced by Terry Melcher: known for his work with The Byrds and Paul Revere and The Raiders. A few months later, the band broke up after Columbia – for whatever reason – shelved the album (which went unreleased until 1992). Cassidy was already long gone at this point, having left the band after injuring his wrist during a performance.

In the meantime, teenagers Jay Ferguson, Randy Wolfe, Mark Andes and Mike Fondiler formed a band called The Red Roosters, and began playing high school dances and small clubs around town. Any momentum the band may have gained was temporarily derailed in April 1966 when Cassidy – who'd married Wolfe's mother Bernice Pearl – moved the family to New York City in search of work. While in the Big Apple, 15-year-old Randy met fellow guitarist Jimmy James at Manny's Music Store. Before he knew it, he was gigging with James and his band The Blue Flames at the infamous Café Wha? in Greenwich Village. James dubbed him Randy California, to distinguish him from band member Randy Palmer (thereafter known as Randy Texas). California picked up more than a few tricks from James, the older musician, who was later to move to England and find fame and fortune after changing his name to Jimi Hendrix.

Randy's family moved back to L.A. in late 1966 – the guitarist rejoining his former bandmates in The Red Roosters. With the addition of his stepfather Cassidy and keyboardist John Locke, they changed the band name to Spirits Rebellious, after a book by spiritual writer Kahlil Gibran. Cassidy was already in his forties at the time – much older than his youthful bandmates – and had decades of experience in the jazz world, playing behind legends like Cannonball Adderley, Thelonious Monk and Roland Kirk.

Locke grew up in a musical household. His father was a classical violinist, and his mother was a composer and opera singer. Also a few years older than his bandmates, Locke had more than a passing familiarity with jazz, and the band's anarchic dynamic allowed him to bring his more-*outré* influence to their signature sound.

By May 1967, they'd dropped the 'Rebellious' from the band name, and became known as just Spirit. Moving into a communal household in Topanga Canyon with roommate Barry Hansen (who later became known as Dr. Demento: the host of a popular weekly syndicated radio program featuring comedy and novelty records), the band honed its musical chemistry by rehearsing daily at the house and performing weekly at L.A. club The Ash Grove: owned by California's uncle Ed Pearl. Randy practically grew up in the club, learning to play guitar from blues legends like Brownie McGhee, Mance Lipscomb and Lightnin' Hopkins, and picking up tips from bluegrass giant Clarence White. As California remembers in the liner notes to the 1996 CD reissue of the band's debut album, 'Many an evening was spent jamming with and learning from these wonderful American artists.'

It was this lineup, with its diverse influences and ideas, that recorded four acclaimed albums between 1967 and 1970. In the wake of their *bona fide* classic *Twelve Dreams Of Dr. Sardonicus*, the band splintered into three notable pieces – Ferguson and Andes to form Jo Jo Gunne, California to pursue a solo career, and Locke and Cassidy trying to keep the Spirit name alive with new musicians – before California eventually reunited with Cassidy and took Spirit as a creative entity, deep into the 1990s, before his tragic death in 1997.

Along the way, the band released several studio albums – most of them quite good and criminally overlooked; a few verging on the greatness displayed by their classic first four LPs. There's a lot to explore here, so we'll begin where the band did: at the Big Yellow House in Topanga Canyon.

Spirit (1968)

Personnel:
Jay Ferguson: vocals, percussion
Randy California: vocals, guitar
Mark Andes: bass, vocals
John Locke: keyboards
Ed Cassidy: drums, percussion
Additional personnel:
Marty Paich: string and horn arrangements
Producer: Lou Adler
Engineers: Eric Wienbang, Armin Steiner, Mike Leitz
Label: Ode Records
Release date: January 1968
Chart position: US: 31
CD reissue produced by Bob Irwin; remixed and mastered by Vic Anesini at Sony Music, NYC
Current editions: US: Sony Legacy Recordings, 2017 (CD), UK: Music On Vinyl, 2019 (LP)

In June 1967, Spirit was playing gigs around the Los Angeles area, looking for a record deal while holding down a regular Monday-night gig at The Ash Grove. The band's friend and roommate Barry Hansen recorded a demo tape of the band, which they shopped to labels around town. They auditioned for producer Lou Adler (The Mamas & the Papas), who'd formed the new label Ode Records, which was distributed by CBS subsidiary Epic Records. He signed Spirit to Ode in August 1967, and rushed them into the studio to record.

Spirit's self-titled debut album was released in January 1968 to a receptive audience. The album was experimental, with an innovative blend of psychedelic rock, blues and folk with jazz undercurrents. *Spirit* spent more than six months on the *Billboard* album chart, peaking at 31: impressive for a debut by an unknown West Coast band. When reissued in 1973 as part of a two-disc set with their 1969 album *Clear*, it inched back into the Top 200 at 191.

While not the band's most influential work, the debut nevertheless inspired a number of musicians, with Led Zeppelin regularly covering 'Fresh Garbage' in concert in their early days, and The C.A. Quintet playing the song for their *Live Trips 1971* album. Art rock band Paranoise reimagined 'Mechanical World' for their 2000 album *Private Power*, while Australian psychedelic outfit Tyrnaround included 'Uncle Jack' on their 2019 compilation *Colour Your Mind*. Artists like Brian Eno and Soft Machine have also cited *Spirit* as an influence.

The album was generally well-received, with Hansen writing a *Rolling Stone* review saying *Spirit* 'is a most uncommon album: one that defies some recent fashions. It's not a frontal assault on the eardrums, and it's not a return to rock and roll. These musicians use their chops in the most imaginative way possible, yet they don't let the experimental tail wag the rocking dog' ... every listen to Spirit – live or recorded – increased my enthusiasm.' Reassessing the album more recently for *All Music Guide*, Richie Unterberger wrote:

> Spirit's debut unveiled a band that seemed determined to out-eclecticize everybody else on the California psychedelic scene, with its mélange of rock, jazz, blues, folk rock, and even a bit of classical and Indian music. Teenaged Randy California immediately established a signature sound with his humming, sustain-heavy tone; middle-aged drummer Ed Cassidy gave the group unusual versatility, and the songs tackled unusual lyrical themes: like 'Fresh Garbage' and 'Mechanical World'. As is often the case in such hybrids, the sum fell somewhat short of the parts – they could play more styles than almost any other group, but couldn't play (or, more crucially, write) as well as the top acts in any given one of those styles.

Spirit also found an early champion in popular BBC radio personality John Peel, who first wrote about the band in his column for *International Times* in 1968. As per the John Peel Wiki, on the 7 February 1970 *Top Gear* show, the influential British DJ mentioned that he'd seen Spirit perform the previous week, calling them 'an amazing band,' and that they were 'perhaps the most impressive band I've ever seen play in my life' before playing their new single '1984'. The band received further UK acclaim from *ZigZag* magazine, while BBC radio host Andy Finney named his Peel-influenced radio program *Fresh Garbage* after the song. CBS Records included the track on the budget compilation *The Rock Machine Turns You On*, which introduced the band in the UK.

In a 2001 interview with publisher Ron Garmon of the zine *Worldly Remains*, Jay Ferguson talked about the band's early sound:

> We were a new category of band, and I think you were hot and cold with Spirit. You either just didn't like it, or you *really* loved it. You had to be open-minded and you had to be ready to take the jazz, because in the beginning, I'd say we were 60% a jazz band, and rock and blues would take up the other 40%. And in the process of that year, the songs began to be written, and we turned into what we were on that first album. But yeah, we were an acquired taste for people.

The debut album wasn't reissued on CD until 1996. As the original 1968 stereo mixes were not available for the CD, the album was remixed, and included four previously-unreleased tracks. In 2017, Audio Fidelity reissued *Spirit* as a limited-edition numbered hybrid Super Audio CD (SACD), which included the original stereo mixes remastered, as the stereo master tape had been found. The SACD release included the same bonus tracks as the 1996 reissue.

'Fresh Garbage' (Ferguson) (3:11)
The song opens with a hypnotic guitar pattern as the other instruments creep in on the edges in lockstep with California's recurring riff. The vocals drift in with a mournful reiteration of the title, as Ferguson swings into the rather simple – albeit effective – lyric:

Look beneath your lid some morning
See the things you didn't quite consume
The world's a can for your fresh garbage

The words are a placeholder for the track's instrumental passages, which are ambitious, inventive, and almost totally without precedent in the rock field in 1968.

If California's succinct guitar patterns weren't exotic enough, Andes adds a hearty bass line, Locke fingers his way across the piano keys with a jazz-flecked solo, and Cass strikes the right balance of light-handed, early-A.M. nightclub brushwork and minor percussion. In the CD liner notes, California said the song was inspired by a garbage strike and the resultant piles of refuse, referring to 'Fresh Garbage' as 'an environmental song ahead of its time!' Writing for UK magazine *Shindig!* in 2009, future Spirit archivist Mick Skidmore said ''Fresh Garbage' encapsulated most of the group's assets within three minutes ... four decades later it hasn't dated at all.'

'Uncle Jack' (Ferguson) (2:44)
Recorded in August 1967 – nearly three months before 'Fresh Garbage' – the British Invasion-styled 'Uncle Jack' sounds like an entirely different band. Evincing a strong UK pop underpinning, the song sounds a lot like the then-burgeoning psychedelic sound of The Move or The Creation to create an infectious earworm. The lyric is pure acid-inspired Summer-of-Love poetry:

Standing there, he's so deceiving
Has he been or is he leaving
Looking in his sea green eyes
Uncle Jack will tell no lies
Can you see it?

Randy's explosive guitar solo ignites the performance, providing a stark counterpoint to the safe-as-milk psych-pop instrumentation and group harmonies. It's an altogether enjoyable song, but miles away from where the band and their debut would finally land.

'Mechanical World' (Andes, Ferguson) (5:15)
Restricted to his room for several weeks while battling an illness, Mark Andes was feeling out-of-touch and somewhat 'mechanical'; his emotions finding their

way into the brilliantly-prescient 'Mechanical World'. The instrumentation is somewhat robotic, with tempo changes, and eerie strings added by arranger Marty Paich.

The lyric is strictly doom and gloom ('Death falls so heavy on my soul/ Death falls so heavy, makes me moan'), but the instrumentation is creative – California's edgy solos right on time; Locke's keyboards finding the darkness in the words and delivery; the song representing the third change of direction in three songs, while presaging the goth and industrial music of the future. Referring California's guitar solo, Ferguson told *Worldly Remains*: 'Randy's solos were these monuments of guitar. They were creations. They were architectural solos, things built on things and developed.'

'Mechanical World' was released as the album's only single, and while not a world-beater, it got the Spirit name out there, and the song became a minor regional hit in pockets across the US.

'Taurus' (California) (2:37)
Ah yes, California's 'Taurus' – a two-and-a-half-minute instrumental that Led Zeppelin *stole*, stretching it into the eight-minute opus that was 'Stairway To Heaven.' I'll get into that controversy in a later chapter, suffice it to say that this too-short electrical shock is simply magical. Opening with Paich's gossamer string arrangement, Randy chimes in with the gorgeous six-string acoustic pattern that informed the opening to 'Stairway'; the charming beauty of his intricate playing and the haunting strings providing the perfect bridge between 'Mechanical World' and the psych-drenched 'Girl In Your Eye.'

'Girl In Your Eye' (Ferguson) (3:15)
The band dips back into the shallow-but-wide psych-rock playbook for this effervescent song – an engaging slice of hippie rock 'n' roll complete with Ferguson's lofty vocals, California's effects-laden sitar-styled guitar, wall-of-sound instrumentation, and just the hint of strings in the background. There's not a lot of meat to Ferguson's lyric ('She's the girl in your eye/Sometimes you wish that you had passed her by/Days come and they go/And if you make it, you just don't know'), but he sells it, and the instrumentation is a showcase for prime-grade lysergic inspiration.

'Straight Arrow' (Ferguson) (2:50)
A fairly straightforward mid-tempo rocker with typical 1960s instrumentation, this nevertheless has moments of true madness, including California's short, shocking solo, which is matched by Andes' rumbling bass notes. The track ends with a proverbial bang; California's discordant fretwork rising to a crescendo with Locke's equally manic keyboard pounding. The song was written about Andes' father, actor Keith Andes after the band saw him play Don Quixote in a stage presentation of *Man of La Mancha,* when they ended up in the same city at the same time while on tour.

'Topanga Windows' (Ferguson) (3:26)

Ferguson emerged as the band's primary songwriter on *Spirit*, penning seven of the eleven songs. If he was still finding his footing as a wordsmith (he was only 20 at the time, after all), he struck gold with the inspired 'Topanga Windows,' which transforms the mundane into pure lyric gold:

> Watching the world through our Topanga window
> Seeing people running through their lives
> Sun shines warm through our Topanga window
> The cat lies sleeping waiting for the night
>
> Your time is going much too fast
> You've got to slow it on down or it won't last
> And what will be will soon enough pass by our Topanga window

Ferguson's vocal is delivered against a mellow backdrop, which becomes a shuffle and grows into a mighty cacophony with California's jaunty solo, Locke's fluid piano and Cassidy's firm hand on the tiller. Sure, it's bog-standard hippie rock, but it rises to the creative standard of contemporaries like Love on the strength of Spirit's talented musicians.

'Gramophone Man' (Ferguson, California, Locke, Andes, Cassidy) (3:49)

The album's only group collaboration was inspired by the band's record-label auditions – the lyric spoofing the industry stereotypes they met. In the CD liner notes, California remembers: 'The executives would come up after our set, pat us on the back and say something like, 'That was very nice, but do you have any songs with a boy-meets-a-girl story line?' Musically it's fairly mundane, save for the middle passage where California plays a jazz solo reminiscent of Larry Carlton or Stan Lassiter, and Cassidy karate-chops his cymbals into submission. The lyric is pretty clever, though:

> And watch the time, the world is waiting
> Give a tune for Mr. gramophone man
> Jack and Jill falling down off their hill
> Singing songs for Mr. gramophone man

'Water Woman' (Ferguson) (2:11)

Ferguson's magnetic 'Water Woman' is one of those boy-meets-girl story songs that record labels wanted at the time, but was perhaps a little too oblique for AM radio. (FM radio didn't become mainstream until 1969, or later depending on where you lived.) Based on a floating nursery-rhyme-style melody, the group vocals, odd sounds and California's complex guitar lines make for an entertaining listen in retrospect.

'The Great Canyon Fire In General' (Ferguson) (2:46)

Throughout *Spirit*, no matter what musical direction the band takes, it's always uniquely Spirit in nature... until this song. Heavily inspired by Jefferson Airplane's genre-defining acid-rock sound (their 'The Ballad Of You And Me And Pooneil' which came out around this time, readily comes to mind), the band add a few flourishes like Locke's spry keyboards and Cassidy's subtle percussive work. Otherwise, California's solos mimic Jefferson Airplane guitarist Jorma Kaukonen, while Andes' bass-playing echoes the Airplane's Jack Casady.

Despite the eerily-similar vocal harmonies, Ferguson's lyric is based on the real-life burning of Topanga Canyon, where the band lived. Their group house was one of the few things left standing in the wildfire's wake.

> Hear the trees crying, all the years dying
> Fire has turned the hills into ashes
> And as the sun ran down from the sky, the canyon burned

'Elijah' (Locke) (10:42)

This extended instrumental jam, closed side two of the original vinyl; California writing in the album liner notes that 'Elijah' became 'Spirit's onstage anthem and trademark. The jazz-like theme was a vehicle for each member to do whatever he wanted during his solo. Some of the more memorable solos I recall were Jay and Mark pulling out two chairs center-stage and facing each other doing the 'Hambone': a two-man hand-slappin', thigh-hittin' rhythmic affair.'

On the record, each instrumentalist is given a chance to shine over the track's ten minutes, and musically the guys are driving all over the road – from Cassidy's machine-gun drum solo to California's clever recurring riff. The song reminds me a lot of The Mothers of Invention's 'The Return Of The Son Of Monster Magnet': a similar improvisation from their 1966 debut album *Freak Out!*

Bonus tracks:

'Veruska' (California) (2:50)

This fierce instrumental performance could've easily found a home on the original album, but was a bonus on the reissue. There are a lot of sounds to digest here, from Randy's razor-sharp Hendrix-inspired fretwork and Locke's creative keyboards, to Cassidy's nuanced percussion. It's a fine production job, with the instruments mixed so that they briefly pan from one speaker to another, creating a mind-bending psychedelic effect.

'Free Spirit' (Locke) (4:27)

Another instrumental, 'Free Spirit,' is more jazz-like than anything on *Spirit*, with Andes' walking bass and Locke's jaunty piano driving what's otherwise an unremarkable performance. California offers some rattletrap guitar, and Cassidy delivers exotic rhythmic percussion, but the various passages just don't flow with the chemistry of 'Elijah' or any of the other lyrical material.

'If I Had A Woman' (California) (3:11)

Sometimes, no matter how hard a band tries, they'll create a song that just doesn't make the cut for an album. This is one such song – with the slightest of lyrics ('If I had a woman/If I had a woman, she'd be mine') and the song lacking any real melody or direction. It's almost as if the entire performance was improvised on the spot as a sort of lark. Though there are some interesting sound effects across the three minutes, the song just never gels.

'Elijah' (Alternate take) (Locke) (9:42)

This alternative rendition of 'Elijah' is only slightly more succinct than the album version – with more avant-garde string-bending from California, a rowdy Andes bass solo, and varying keyboard patterns. If the album version sparked memories of The Mothers of Invention, this alternate take brings to mind later experimental guitarists like Eugene Chadbourne, Fred Frith or Marc Ribot, while Locke's jazz keyboard runs range from bebop to fusion. This performance is altogether more ambitious and weird than the album version, but both display the band's enormous instrumental talents and still-maturing collective imagination.

While they were making a name for themselves, Spirit – like many Los Angeles-based bands – played a lot of low-profile shows in the Southern California area: in high-school gyms and VFW halls. The band defied expectations, even in those early days. In an interview with *Ugly Things* magazine's Bruno Ceriotti, singer Bill Sheppard of L.A. band Stack recalled an interesting interlude when opening for Spirit at a 1968 show at a local high school:

Apparently, I appeared nervous about a different issue that night, because following our soundcheck, Randy California politely came up to me out of nowhere and said, 'Hey kid, you look nervous, wanna get mellow?' I said, 'Sure, mellow sounds real good right now!' So he took me up on the stage, behind the screen for the light-show projector, and opened up a guitar case and pulled out a couple of badminton rackets and a birdie. He handed me a racket and pointed, 'Stand over there.' I got about 15 feet away from him, and he hit the birdie to me, beginning a volley that lasted about five or ten minutes, and then he said, 'That should do it. Have a good show!' He collected his badminton gear and went on about his business. Indeed, it worked perfectly, we had a great show! I'll always be grateful for him showing me his compassion and wisdom. Thanks, Randy!

The Family That Plays Together (1968)

Personnel:
Jay Ferguson: vocals, percussion
Randy California: vocals, guitar
Mark Andes: bass, vocals
John Locke: keyboards
Ed Cassidy: drums, percussion
Additional personnel:
Marty Paich: string and horn arrangements
Marshall Blonstein: additional dialogue
Producer: Lou Adler
Engineers: Eric Wienbang, Armin Steiner
Label: Ode Records
Release date: December 1968
Chart position: US: 22
CD reissue produced by Bob Irwin; remixed and mastered by Vic Anesini at Sony Music, NYC
Current edition: US: Sony Legacy Recordings, 2017 (CD), UK: Music On Vinyl, 2019 (LP)

The modest success of *Spirit* raised expectations for *The Family That Plays Together,* which, it could be argued, delivered in spades. Though much of the album shows only a slight expansion on the debut's sonic blueprint, it displays a more fully-integrated band chemistry, crafting songs that still experimented with psychedelia, folk, blues and jazz alongside their hardwired hard rock sound. But did so with a slightly more radio-friendly sound, with more than half the album (six songs) running to only three minutes or less in length (compared with five such songs on the debut).

They scored a top-30 hit with 'I Got A Line On You': a melodic gem still receiving significant classic rock radio airplay more than 50 years later. The hit helped push sales of the album, which peaked at 22 in *Billboard*. Randy wrote in the reissue liner notes:

What a wonderful gift we all shared that summer of 1969. 'I Got A Line On You' became a big hit, and propelled us to headline status. Some of the groups that opened up for us that year were Chicago, Led Zeppelin and Traffic. We also played the Atlanta Pop Festival for over 100,000 people, and I got the chance to meet up again with my old guitar buddy Jimi Hendrix.

The album title was derived from California's relationship with his stepfather, and from the band's communal household in Topanga Canyon. Randy wrote in the liner notes: 'At the time, the entire group – including wives, girlfriends and siblings – shared one big yellow house … this beautiful rural setting provided the perfect respite and creative backdrop, not only for Spirit but for

Canned Heat, Neil Young and Buffalo Springfield.' Further exploring the band's living conditions, California remembered: 'The upstairs living room – whose windows overlooked Topanga Creek and a beautiful sunlit oak tree – was also our designated rehearsal hall. It was there, five days a week, that the band got together to explore, experiment, share, offer support for each other's ideas, and most of all, feel the joy of letting go and becoming as one: family.'

The album cover was photographed at the Sunset Highland Hotel on Sunset Boulevard in Hollywood, across the street from Hollywood High School, which boasts among its famous alumni, musicians like Lowell George (Little Feat), Ricky Nelson, and legendary Los Angeles DJ Don Steele.

The album received a fair amount of critical acclaim, with Hansen writing in his *Rolling Stone* review that it 'is a wide-ranging exploration of the rock universe. Jazz, classical, country, blues and plain old rock all contribute to Spirit's sound'. He noted the band's maturation, and especially Ferguson's increased vocal prowess, stating, 'A good year on the road has turned Jay Ferguson – the boyish voice on the first album – into a first-rate lead singer.' As he did with his *Spirit* review, Hansen concluded, 'Spirit has a unique combination of imagination and taste – the ability to create fresh sounds, plus a keen feeling for proportion.'

In an interview with *Shindig!* writer Mick Skidmore, Jay Ferguson recalled *The Family That Plays Together* as 'a super record,' and praised his bandmate, saying, 'That was really Randy's coming out. He was writing songs, singing and playing with dynamic energy.'

In his 1983 overview of the band's career for the UK magazine *The History of Rock*, Max Bell wrote of 'I Got A Line On You':

> This demonstration of their poppier side proved that the group couldn't be categorized in any particular style – a quality that, in the end, was to undermine their chances of sustaining commercial success. Although their first two albums each sold in excess of 200,000 copies, Spirit never attained the heights of popularity their music merited, despite being respected by peers and critics alike.

As with *Spirit*, the original stereo master tape was unavailable for the Sony CD and subsequent vinyl reissue on Bob Irwin's Sundazed Records, which instead used new stereo mixes by Irwin, California and Cassidy. The tracks that appeared for the first time on the *Time Circle, 1968-1972* compilation were provided mixes different from the CD reissues, but the 2017 Audio Fidelity limited-edition SACD reissue worked from the original 1968 stereo master.

'I Got A Line On You' (California) (2:37)

Randy California's bluesy rocker offered plenty of everything needed for the upcoming FM radio explosion – his incendiary fretwork, a solid bass riff, unison vocals and a melodic hook that you could hang your hat. This all earned Spirit their first *bona fide* hit. The song is also a perfect showcase for their growing musical chemistry; the inspired production manages to fit all the disparate instrumental pieces into a coherent whole. And while California's lyrics are nothing to write home about (It's a love song, of sorts), it's the innovative sound and dynamic performance that hold it together.

The single was released ahead of the album in October 1968, and slowly climbed the chart to peak at #25 five months later. Several international versions of the single were released in late 1968 and early 1969 – some on collectible psychedelic-colored vinyl – and it quickly became one of the band's signature songs. It had staying power, too, being covered over the years by talents as diverse as southern rockers Blackfoot, Nashville art rockers Chagall Guevara, Rock and Roll Hall of Famer Alice Cooper, Canadian bluesman Jeff Healey, and Kim Mitchell of the Canadian band Max Webster. Even Spirit *covered* the song on their final reunion album *The Thirteenth Dream*, in 1984.

'It Shall Be' (California, Locke) (3:25)

'I Got A Line On You' segues beautifully into the slower 'It Shall Be', Locke's discordant piano riff walking the listener through the intro; the deceptively alluring instrumentation gliding along on the magic of Marty Paich's string arrangement. Though Paich loaded the arrangement with more horns than necessary – swinging wildly from R&B/soul to jazz blasts – the melodic flute weaving in and out provides a suitable ambiance recalling Herbie Mann's work.

The lyrics are undoubtedly Randy California's, and speak of the 1960s' ethos of peace and brotherhood: 'In the future soon, beauty will find you and all of mankind/Together binding you and me.' In the CD liner notes, Randy wrote: 'I felt inspired to write hopeful lyrics, at a time when many guys our age were being sent to Vietnam. It is very compelling when vets come up to me today and say things like how much Spirit's music meant to them and how it helped get them through a very dangerous time.' Though 'It Shall Be' is a whiplash change-of-pace from the album opener, it's a nice reminder of the band's innovative songwriting.

'Poor Richard' (Ferguson) (2:29)

Recalling the first album's 'Fresh Garbage,' this opens with Andes' bass throbbing, before breaking into vocal harmonies that rest uneasily atop California's scratchy guitar work, Locke's hidden-in-the-mix piano, Cassidy's steady rhythm and Andes' dominant bass riff. The vocals mimic those n 'Fresh Garbage' in phrasing and meter, while the lyric builds on the earlier song's environmental message:

Remarking on the freshness of garbage
With each and every person that he meets
And debating on the price of admission

While someone is lying, dying in the street
Notwithstanding all the manner of people
The city you'll find is such a lonely place to live and live and live

Many of the album's songs lead one into the other with the barest of breaks, and have a shared instrumentation tying them together thematically. California's guitars were double-tracked, giving the song a more massive, mind-blowing signature.

'Silky Sam' (Ferguson) (4:06)

Psychedelic rock was already evolving into something else entirely by 1969, and while Spirit's debut album had wandered through the genre sparingly, their musical identity wasn't tied to psychedelia like so many late-1960s bands. Where some groups (The Pretty Things come to mind) struggled to transcend their psych rock roots, others (like Pink Floyd) took the lessons they'd learned from the era and used their newfound freedom to explore other musical directions. 'Silky Sam' is Spirit's bridge from 1960s-era psych rock to an equally mind-blowing sound they'd explore at length on *Twelve Dreams Of Dr. Sardonicus*.

Ferguson's intriguing lyric makes for an interesting character study, based on the band's promo person Marshall Blonstein, who is included on the recording in a brief spoken-word segment: 'Silky Sam was a gambling man, and the cards all would dance in his hand. The stars would shine just to make a lucky sign, so you'd understand.' The protagonist's sadness reflects that of Pagliacci in Smokey Robinson's classic 'Tears Of A Clown.' While the minimalist backing track is ever-ascending, there are Beatlesque melodic breaks, and about halfway through, a noisy discordant passage featuring Locke's jarring piano and Cassidy's crashing rhythms.

'Drunkard' (Ferguson) (2:38)

Another oblique Ferguson story, 'Drunkard' is a delightfully-chaotic mess musically, with oddball instrumental passages, interludes of light and dark, mourning strings (Paich gets a little carried away with the weeping violins at times), moments of pure melancholy and cacophonous cries of joy, all crammed into two and a half minutes. Ferguson seems to be singing of a man full of doubt, searching for something he'd never find:

His coat was torn and tattered
His face was full of red
And nothing seemed to matter as he put himself to bed
And he didn't know the meaning of it all

Once again, the notes pouring out of a lonely flute help create an appropriate ambiance for the song's lyrical angst.

'Darlin' If' (Ferguson) (3:38)

Not quite a ballad, but in the same ballpark, this is an unabashed love song driven by Ferguson's plaintive vocal and Locke's emotional piano playing. California adds a gorgeous guitar solo in the middle, and while Paich's strings add a certain romance, I can't help but think the song would've been better had they continued along the lines of Ferguson's rising vocal phrasing and simply rocked out for the last 45 seconds or so.

'It's All The Same' (California, Cassidy) (4:40)

It's not a Spirit album without a touch of their trademark weirdness, and this song plays that role on this album. Opening with the effect of what sounds like a spaceship landing, the track chugs in on the wings of California's jagged guitar licks and Andes' funky bass line. The performance has plenty of energy, with California's lyric searching for a certain spiritual awakening in an uncertain era:

> Someone here will try and waste your time
> And someone there will try and lead you blind
> Life seems to be wandering 'round and 'round
> Searching for the that which can be found

Cassidy delivers a short, sharp drum solo mid-song, but it's the catchy chorus ('It's you, you, you/It's me, me, me/It's you and me, babe/We're all the same') that elevates the song to pop status – friendly enough for AM radio, but edgy enough for FM if the label had released it as a single.

'Jewish' (California) (2:48)

This lyric is entirely in Hebrew, and was derived from the traditional Hebrew song 'Hine Ma Tov,' which was based on King David's Psalm 133 with its line 'How pleasant it is for brethren to dwell together,' so it seems to be a nod to the band's friendship and the album title. Musically, 'Jewish' is quite exciting, offering varying guitar patterns, including one monster circular riff and three-part harmonies, accompanied by Cassidy's drum accents.

'Dream Within A Dream' (Ferguson) (3:01)

Opening with Ferguson's vocal, with the band's backing harmonies and Locke's piano leads, this explodes into what could be a *Sgt. Pepper's*-style outtake, with an adventurous melody and California's livewire guitar-playing. Ferguson's lyric still displays a hint of psychedelia, even if the listener isn't sure of the point he's trying to make: 'Stepping off this mortal coil will be my pleasure/Giving the gift that giving brings to be my pleasure.' The words are delivered with sincerity, against a strong instrumental backdrop. Based on its energy alone, the song could have become an FM radio hit had it not arrived several months early to take advantage of the new format.

'She Smiles' (Ferguson) (2:30)

It seems like Spirit really *were* trying to write a few more *traditional* songs to fit into the label execs' preferred market. By late 1968, AM radio was beginning to stretch out and experiment with bold new songs; the format's inherent conservatism nevertheless making room for hit singles by The Doors, The Beatles, Cream and Sly and the Family Stone, among others receiving significant airplay that year. 'She Smiles' is dressed for success, with a short running time, haunting guitar work, an earnest vocal, the slightest radio-friendly melody, and psych-influenced lyrics: 'Look at her there/She's sitting in her comfortable chair/The flowers slipping down through her hair/She smiles.' The song is about growing old with grace and dignity; the girl from the opening verse is now an old woman who 'lets the music run from her hands.' It's a clever lyric construct and a gorgeous song overall.

'Aren't You Glad' (Ferguson) (5:31)

As he did with the debut album, Ferguson takes the songwriting lead on this album, penning seven songs, but allowing the entire band to imbue each performance with their own individual fingerprint. Nowhere on the album is this more apparent than on the closer 'Aren't You Glad.' But honestly, the lyric is a trifle. The main words are 'Aren't you glad you're glad you're glad baby/ Yes I'm glad so glad I'm that baby,' but they're delivered with a mesmerizing cadence, underscored by California's charismatic leads. Paich layers in uncharacteristically subtle strings, and the players contribute their individual textures.

There are a few solos included in the track's five minutes-plus, but nothing too audacious or ambitious; Adler's warm production and the up-tempo finale ending the album on a high note. In the CD liner notes, California said the song 'typifies what Spirit was all about, with and for each other. Often when a song was finished, someone would start it up again, and the whole band would join in. We did this all the time at rehearsals and live performances.'

On the subject of his songs dominating the first two albums, Ferguson told *Worldly Remains* zine:

I think the rest of the band, as songwriters, really hadn't found their styles yet. The rest of the band was more coming from the school of improvisation and jazz, and we'd do an old song and do our take on it ... and in those early songs, I would try to showcase the different styles of the players ... my attempt as a songwriter was to try and reflect all those styles.

Bonus tracks
'Fog' (Locke, California) (2:24)

Spirit evidently recorded a lot of instrumental tracks that never saw release at the time – 'Fog' arriving as a bonus track on the album's 1996 Sony CD reissue. A moody, somewhat exotic performance built around Locke's ethereal keyboards, Cassidy's tribal drum rhythms and Paich's thinly-spun string arrangement, it's a provocative composition – almost classical in nature – that could've easily been slotted in between two of the album's more up-tempo songs.

'So Little To Say' (Ferguson, 2:59)
One of Ferguson's lesser songs, this is built around Locke's piano and keyboards; Paich's string arrangement adds punch. There's a nice California solo about two minutes in, but the vocal is slight and unconvincing, the entire performance too saccharine by half, with too many horns for my liking.

'Mellow Fellow' (Locke) (3:48)
This is a sort of harbinger of things to come and 1969's *Clear* album. A vaguely Brazilian rhythm is surrounded by Locke's minimalist piano notes, Cassidy's light brushwork and syncopated drum rhythm, and California's resounding guitar solos. It's jazz-like, but veers dangerously close to the pioneering jazz-rock fusion sound.

'Now Or Anywhere' (Ferguson) (4:21)
A plodding hard rocker with heavy instrumentation, this presages Black Sabbath and Led Zeppelin, with discordant, riff-happy guitars, feedback, clomping drums and off-kilter vocals. While it's obviously experimental in nature, it's too clamorous to play well with the album's original sequencing (thus its omission, perhaps).

'Space Chile' (Locke) (6:26)
This extended instrumental featuring Locke's immense keyboard skills, sounds rather *new age*, flying awfully close to the sun with a space-music vibe, save for Cassidy's unexpected and – frankly – unneeded drum solo, and California's wonky string-bending. This smells a lot like a jam caught on tape, with a meandering song structure, and little or no end point in sight; just a fade out and a fade away from memory. It's interesting, but not a performance that commands repeated play.

Randy California wrote in May 1996: 'They say that blood is thicker than water, and I can tell you it was the feeling of our family connection that gave Spirit its unique character and strength in 1969.' Though this fellowship was to fracture in the future, it held steady through two more classic albums.

Clear (1969)

Personnel:
Jay Ferguson: vocals, percussion
Randy California: vocals, guitar
Mark Andes: bass, vocals
John Locke: keyboards
Ed Cassidy: drums, percussion
Additional personnel:
Marty Paich: string and horn arrangements
Producer: Lou Adler
Engineers: Eric Wienbang, Armin Steiner, John Stachowaik
Label: Ode Records
Release date: September 1969
Chart position: US: 55
CD reissue produced by Bob Irwin; remixed by Vic Anesini at Sony Music, NYC
Current editions: US: Sony Legacy Recordings, 2017 (CD), UK: Eastworld
Recordings, 2013 (CD)

Spirit's third album *Clear* is widely considered to be the least of their classic
first four, and was a rush job that came in the wake of releasing two LPs the
previous year and working on the soundtrack to the 1969 film *Model Shop*
(more about which later). The band felt there wasn't enough time to perfect
the songs on *Clear*.

The label seems to have still been standing in Spirit's corner at this time,
landing them the soundtrack gig, and pushing them into the studio to record
the follow-up to the modestly successful *The Family That Plays Together*.
Expectations were raised again, and a hit along the lines of 'I Got A Line On
You' was going to be necessary to sustain continued label interest. But *Clear*
slipped commercially, peaking at 55 in *Billboard* and failing to yield a hit
single. The sole single – the trippy and engaging 'Dark Eyed Woman' – was
good enough to succeed but just didn't get enough promotional juice to push
it past the finish line.

The band's management and record label both dropped the ball. Randy
California said in the *Clear* CD liner notes:

> Spirit was offered the spot right before Jimi Hendrix at the Woodstock pop
> festival. Instead, it was decided to send Randy California, Jay Ferguson, Ed
> Cassidy, Mark Andes, and John Locke on a radio promo tour. Needless to say,
> Spirit was a no-show at the biggest rock and roll event ever. You can imagine
> how we all felt watching Woodstock on the 5 o'clock news, knowing we should
> have been there.

While there's no way of knowing what a Woodstock appearance might've done
for the band's fortunes, it's unlikely to have hurt them. Continuing, Randy said,

'People often come up and ask the question, 'Why didn't Spirit make it big?' For this reason – and to set the record straight – I felt it necessary to tell this story.' The rush to record *Clear*, and the pressure to get a follow-up hit single, clearly weighed heavily on the band, California saying, 'This was a very trying time for the band, and what transpired during this period seemed to plant the seeds of our breakup in 1971.'

With an uneven slate of songs, *Clear* received a mixed critical response. In the *Village Voice*, critic Robert Christgau said Spirit are 'a talented group with guts of cellophane. Randy California is the rock equivalent of the cool, progressive jazzman of the '50s. The group can be very good – side one is mostly excellent rock – and incredibly empty.' I have to agree somewhat – much of the good stuff on *Clear* is on side one, with half of side two comprised of (mostly) ill-conceived instrumentals. In my original review of the 1996 CD reissue, I wrote, 'The tension is evident on *Clear*, the music displaying a harder edge than their previous works, rocking with abandon and more force than they'd shown before. The political turmoil of the country at large is evident on *Clear*, with cuts like 'Policeman's Ball' and 'So Little Time To Fly' showcasing a newfound social awareness.' But there are hints of the band's future in these grooves, which partially redeems the album's dashed-off nature.

'Dark Eyed Woman' (California, Ferguson) (3:07)

Anticipating the trippy, hippie dreamlike haze they'd create on *Twelve Dreams of Dr. Sardonicus*, this opens with a short intro before Randy's wicked riff jumps out, Andes' razor-sharp bass licks lay deep in the cut, and Locke's keyboards fill out the sound. California's mid-song solo is all fang and claw: the guitarist ripping at the strings while a discordant piano squawks in the background. The lyric isn't too bad either:

> Dark eyed woman on a hot summer's night
> Dark eyed woman are you burning tonight?
> Dark eyed woman won't you step in the light

They're delivered with a touch of mystery, while the band rages behind the vocal. It was released as a single, but label promotion must've been minimal, as it could've been an FM-radio bullseye.

'Apple Orchard' (California, Ferguson, Andes, Cassidy, Locke) (4:07)

Another group collaboration; it's not so much the singing here, but rather the *way* it's sung.

> I've been working in the orchard
> I've been pulling down the apples all day
> I've been looking at your daughter
> And I've been thinking about most of the way

It seems to be a tale of forbidden migrant love – steam from the lusty vocal bubbling up from the groove. The soundtrack is A-grade psych-drenched hard rock, with syncopated rhythms, dancing bass lines and enough hot licks to shank your eardrums into oblivion with every listen.

'So Little Time To Fly' (California, Locke) (2:49)
Randy California was the king of the (possibly) postdated flower-child lyric, and this was no exception – another song about getting back to the country and finding peace and brotherhood: 'Find a garden that's green all year/And you might not have to hear the sound the city is calling.' California's guitar part is a bit more raucous than your typical hippie rock ode of the era, with a couple of distinctive and different solos, while each band member meanders in their own individual direction instrumentally. Yet somehow, it all meshes together into a lovely performance.

'Ground Hog' (Ferguson) (3:04)
How many songs have been written about the humble groundhog in the history of rock 'n' roll? My guess would be less than the fingers on one hand, yet here's Mr. Ferguson whipping up a reasonably clever love song around Groundhog Day, singing, 'Well, I hope you don't find no shadow 'round your hole when you're trying to look over your shoulder,' and his gal won't be marrying him until spring rolls around. The seemingly inane lyric is almost overwhelmed by the pig-iron strength of the backing track, starting with California's country blues picking, vocal harmonies and Mark Andes' mauling his four strings like his bass is the lead instrument. Some elements – like the dynamic guitar-and-bass interplay – would be more fully fleshed-out on the next album. In the reissue liner notes, Ferguson said the song 'touches on some of my earliest roots. My very first band played Appalachian and mountain music; I played 5-string banjo. 'Ground Hog' was kind of a deep-holler chant, done Spirit style.'

'Cold Wind' (Ferguson) (3:24)
This obligatory ballad – though one of the album's weaker links – is an otherwise gorgeous song searching for a melodic hook to hang onto. John Locke's piano intro resembles that from Bill Withers' 'Lean On Me'. The group harmonies don't help their case here, mimicking Locke's elegant piano playing. The song itself wanders all over the place, and while they are fine instrumental performances, it never coalesces into a coherent whole. Even Randy's solo near the end sounds like it was tacked on at the last minute.

'Policeman's Ball' (Ferguson) (2:21)
At first, Locke's lively piano intro sounds like he's leading into a torch song, but then the rhythm becomes jaunty, and the oddball instrumentation blares from your speakers like you were just dropped from a great height, headfirst into a carnival tent. Ending side one, it's an upbeat song, but jarringly incongruous

(like peanut butter and jelly sold in the same jar). In the CD liner notes, Ferguson says the song 'was really a reaction to what happened during the Chicago Democratic convention in '68. The police showed their dark side; all this pent-up anger just exploded. This song was a satire on a certain kind of mentality, done almost with Jim Kweskin jug-band style.'

'Ice' (Locke) (5:52)
Side two opened with this staid John Locke instrumental – a prog-like avant-garde jam that recalls The Mothers of Invention, but maybe with more pomp-and-circus-pants instrumentation. While the individual performances are impressive, it too frequently wanders off while looking for somewhere to land. Cassidy's underlying percussion work is pretty nifty, even if the track is about twice as long as it needed to be.

'Give A Life, Take A Life' (California, Adler) (3:23)
I'm not sure what producer Lou Adler brought to the table for this – the only Spirit song he earned a writing credit for – but this co-write with California is a mere trifle. With lofty, floating vocals, baroque-sounding piano and ridiculous vocal harmonies, it's side two's second dud in a row.

'I'm Truckin'' (Locke) (2:25)
This is more like it, sounding like something Ferguson or California might've come up with. It's a mid-tempo slab of rock with staggered vocals, swaggering guitar licks, slap-happy bass and solid percussion, with a lyric that makes one wonder what John was smoking/ingesting at the time:

> Twenty years went by, I couldn't decide
> I took a little ride, I rode it like a siren
> Water was fine, I had a great time
> I nearly went blind, seeing all that lightning

It's a fine hard rocker by the standards of the time, and fits into a hallowed hippie-rock tradition of songs built on the youthful concept of movement, time and place: best captured by the Grateful Dead's classic 'Truckin'.'

'Clear' (California, Ferguson) (4:09)
The third of the album's three instrumentals is more jazz-like and classy than its brethren, concentrating on California's mesmerizing six-string work and Locke's symphonic backdrop. They could have shaved 30 seconds or so from it, but it's fine, especially compared to what comes after...

'Caught' (Locke) (3:10)
You know the band was out of ideas when they got to this point on the record. Locke can't seem to make up his mind iwhat direction he wants to take the song

in. It starts out sounding like Saturday night at the honky-tonk, before veering across Kurt Weill's gutter-cabaret turf, finally landing on a tepid jazz groove. It's a throwaway that wouldn't have even merited inclusion as a future bonus track.

'New Dope In Town' (Andes, California, Cassidy, Ferguson, Locke) (4:24)

Released as the B-side to 'Dark Eyed Woman', this schizoid song can't make up its mind what it is: the band grasping at any buoy floating in a sea of possibilities. There's more of the wretched piano-popping cabaret sound of 'Caught' along with some improvised jazz, whimsical lyrics delivered whimsically, and a bit of fringe guitar – none of which ever fits together in the band's usual cohesion.

Bonus Tracks
'1984' (California) (3:37)

It's a shame the orphan single '1984' wasn't written in time to have been included on *Clear*: the song recorded a month after the album's release. Appearing as a single in February 1970 between the *Clear* release and the making of *Twelve Dreams Of Dr. Sardonicus* – '1984' inched its way to 69 on the charts but didn't appear on album until *The Best of Spirit* in 1973. After some initial FM-radio airplay, the song was pulled from station playlists for being too political. It should've gone a lot further than it did. One of California's better songs, its prescient lyric echoes as loudly today as it did in 1970:

> 1984, knockin' on your door
> Will you let it come?
> Will you let it run your life?
>
> Plexi-plastic eyeball, he's your special friend,
> He sees you every night
> Well he calls himself Big Brother
> But you know it's no game
> You're never out of his sight

The track opens with a barrage of percussion courtesy of Mr. 'Big Beat' Cassidy; the strident group vocals giving way to the lyric, which marches in step with California's sledgehammer riff and Locke's psychedelic keyboard washes. Randy's solo at 2:27 could cut bone, Cassidy keeps time with his percussive bombing runs, and the undeniable chorus pounds your cerebellum like a migraine. With the least bit of label promo effort, it could've been a huge FM hit.

'Sweet Stella Baby' (Ferguson) (2:55)

Another sweet enigma here. This was the B-side of the '1984' single, recorded the day after, and itself is an A-side-worthy track. Ferguson's vocal is high-energy and inspired, the group harmonies are perfect, Locke's piano dances in step with the vocals, while Cassidy delivers an imaginative rhythmic backbone. As usual, Randy's solos are creative and evocative.

'Fuller Brush Man' (Ferguson) (3:19)

Here's one that never made it off the launch pad. It's as lyrically inane as 'Apple Orchard,' but with a bizarre vocal that sounds like the singer is putting us on. It's a shame, as the playing is quite fetching, with flamethrower fretwork, tasty piano, brash cymbal work, and Andes' typically-underrated bass-playing. The band seldom revisited the song in later days, though it did appear on *Eventide*: the Sundazed compilation of oddities and rarities.

Critic Matthew Greenwald of *AllMusic* saw the song in a similar light:

> A somewhat strange falsetto vocal opening from Jay Ferguson opens up this Spirit oddity, which (rightfully) went unreleased until the 1996 *Clear* reissue by Sony/Legacy. It's a colorful portrait of human nature and the title subject. The actual verses and chorus are more in keeping with the band's refined elegance, sounding not unlike their 'Dream Within A Dream': a standout from *The Family That Plays Together*. In the end, it's really only for completists.

'Coral' (Locke, Cassidy) (3:05)

Originally recorded for the *Model Shop* soundtrack, this outtake is more fully orchestrated, the concept carried further than on the film version. Sporting provocative instrumentation, it's a fine display of the band's musical chemistry – all the gears meshing as one symmetrical machine, the result a sensitive yet spry instrumental that does a fair job of creating a particular cinematic mood. The song was dedicated to Coral Shields – the younger sister of legendary L.A. groupie Sable Starr, whom Randy was dating at the time. After a false stop and a few seconds, 'Coral' leads into a vintage album promo that would've run on FM stations across the country at the time.

Twelve Dreams Of Dr. Sardonicus (1970)

Personnel:
Jay Ferguson: vocals, percussion, keyboards
Randy California: vocals, guitar, bass
Mark Andes: bass, vocals
John Locke: keyboards, synthesizer, art direction
Ed Cassidy: drums, percussion
Additional personnel:
Matt Andes: dobro ('Nothin' To Hide')
David Blumberg: horn arrangements
Producer: David Briggs
Label: Epic Records
Release date: November 1970
Chart position: US: 63
CD reissue produced by Bob Irwin; remixed and mastered by Vic Anesini at Sony
Music, NYC
Current edition US: Sundazed Music, 2009 (LP); UK: Esoteric Recordings, 2022 (CD)

This most enduring of Spirit's many albums is considered their masterpiece. Curiously, as of this writing, the CD is out of print in the US, though copies of the 1996 reissue are readily available on the Discogs website and elsewhere. Esoteric Recordings in the UK released an expanded CD version with bonus live tracks in early 2022.

Twelve Dreams is where everything great about Spirit came together at one time – the stars aligning under producer David Briggs' guiding hand, coaxing magnificent from a band in the process of fracturing. Briggs came to Spirit by way of his friendship with singer/songwriter Neil Young; the pair eventually working together on over a dozen albums. Briggs also produced artists as diverse as Willie Nelson, Nils Lofgren, Nick Cave and Tom Rush, among others.

After recording three albums with label executive and producer Lou Adler, California had his eye on Briggs. In the CD reissue liner notes, he remembers:

One spring morning in 1970, I paid a visit to Neil Young at his mountaintop wooden home in Topanga. The purpose of that visit was to inquire about David Briggs as a possible producer for Spirit's next album. The recommendation from Neil was 100% yes! I then drove to the bottom of the canyon, met up with David, and henceforth began a relationship that would produce – in many people's opinion – Spirit's finest creation to date.

Briggs turned out to be an inspired choice. He was only a couple of years older than Ferguson and Andes, and was part of the 1960s generation of free-thinking artistes. Adler was a decade older than the band (but a decade *younger* than Cassidy!), and though he was a deft hand at producing pop-rock acts like The Mamas & The Papas, Spirit was moving into a more adventurous, almost art-rock direction. California wrote: 'During the five months we took recording *Twelve Dreams Of Dr. Sardonicus*, David became a sixth member of the band. Acting as a catalyst and friend, David inspired and guided us to our very best studio performances. I will always remember him for his quick wit, no-nonsense decisions and brotherly disposition.' Indeed, Briggs helped Spirit hone the sounds they'd previously explored, and captured the band's performances with more energy and electricity than Adler ever did.

Sadly – even with a new producer pumping new life into the band's sound, *Twelve Dreams* underperformed commercially, putting Spirit under further pressure to deliver a hit. *Twelve Dreams* peaked at 63 in *Billboard*. The album's three singles – 'Animal Zoo', 'Nature's Way' and 'Mr. Skin' – barely scraped the Hot 100. But the album's reputation and fortunes grew over the years, it being certified Gold in 1976, for more than 500,000 records sold.

Twelve Dreams garnered a mixed critical response. In his popular Consumer Guide for *The Village Voice*, Robert Christgau wrote:

Both Randy California and the band have their own cool, rich, jazzy style – a genuine achievement. But that doesn't mean you have to like it. They play better than they write, and since they still play songs, that's a problem. A worse problem is that the lyrics are rarely as cerebral as the music.

Nevertheless, Christgau proffered the album a grade of B.

With tongue partially in his cheek, critic Nick Tosches down-rated the album in *Rolling Stone*, writing, 'To badmouth this LP on account of its shortcomings, is like chastizing the child for watering the rhubarb but forgetting to buy the bacon: such, in sooth, are its apexes.'

The album has received more acclaim as the years have rolled by. Richie Unterberger wrote in his AllMusic reappraisal: 'Although *Twelve Dreams Of Dr. Sardonicus* has the reputation of being Spirit's most far-out album, it actually contains the most disciplined songwriting and playing of the original lineup; cutting back on some of the drifting, and offering some of their more melodic tunes.'

In *The History of Rock*, Max Bell wrote:

California and Ferguson had differing ideas on which way their music should develop. Their final album as a five-piece was recorded under acrimonious and bizarre circumstances, but in retrospect, was their most overtly commercial work. Indeed *The Twelve Dreams Of Dr. Sardonicus* – released in 1970 – has since been hailed as Spirit's masterpiece, with its hallucinogenic tone reflected by David Briggs' production.

Cult critic 'Ranger Reek' Johnson wrote about early-Spirit for *Creem* magazine in February 1974:

They sure were a great band, too, piling Jay's bizzarro flagellation numbers on top of Randy California's comatose it's-not-nice-to-fool-Mother-Nature eco-rants on top of Lou Adler's Mantovanoid-creamed string readymades on top of Moog instrumental fakeouts that might have sounded futuristic in the '50s' ... no doubt about it, Spirit had what it takes. If any particular excess of theirs wasn't up your alley, you could be sure they'd eventually hit your own personal dimwit heaven, and you'd sop it up like the cretinous sponge farm everybody really wants to be.

In his *Classic Rock* magazine review of the 2022 *Twelve Dreams* CD reissue, Paul Moody wrote, 'First released in November 1970, Spirits fourth album remains one of the most fearlessly inventive records to emerge during that hallowed decade ... overall this is the perfect place to start investigations into the Spirit world.'

In my review of the 1996 CD reissue, I wrote: 'An inspired mix of every musical trick that Spirit had in their considerable arsenal of skills, *Twelve Dreams* stands up decades later as one of the classic rock recordings of all time ... mixing their improvisational backgrounds with a traditional three-and-a-half-minute rock song structure, the band created music that was chaotic genius.'

'Prelude – Nothin' To Hide' (California) (3:43)

'Prelude' rests on Randy's elegant acoustic guitar – a pastoral opening setting the stage for what seems to be another ecologically-minded song:

> You have the world at your fingertips
> No one can make it better than you
> You have the world at your fingertips
> But see what you've done to the rain and the sun

Then the electric guitar comes through, the rhythm gets big and funky, and the band rips into 'Nothin' To Hide', which is an entirely different sort of song, with nonsensical lysergic-draped lines like 'Swastika plug in your wear/Jealous stars in your pants' and 'Drink it down, a jug full of beer/The bloated heads in your hands.'

If this isn't a heavy-enough trip for you, 'Nothin' To Hide' swerves around a corner and kicks into high gear slightly more than halfway through, as jagged shards of guitar lead the way into horn-fueled anarchy – the instruments panned from one speaker to the other, as a mutant mariachi band plays in the background, all semblance of vocal cohesion lost, and the overall cacophony hiding some mighty-fine playing as the song finally swirls to a satisfying conclusion. According to California in the CD liner notes, the phrase 'Married to the same bride' refers to the 'love of the music which we all shared', and that his idea for the song 'found its way into my heart one afternoon, sitting down by Topanga Creek.'

'Nature's Way' (California) (2:40)

Randy gets back to the ecology anthem he started with 'Prelude', in the classic 'Nature's Way'. Eschewing the oblique lyric style of most songs of this ilk in favor of a more straightforward approach, the music is mid-tempo with peaks of clamorous instrumentation; Randy's guitar riding the waves like a surfer, and the group harmonies giving the lyric, gravitas: –

It's nature's way of telling you something's wrong
It's nature's way of telling you in a song

It's nature's way of telling you, it's in the breeze
It's nature's way of telling you, dying trees

The lyric isn't overly complicated, and Randy's plaintive vocal perfectly fits the message. He went into more depth on the songwriting in the CD liner notes:

I wrote this song up in San Francisco while doing a gig at the Fillmore West. Written in the afternoon, I can't remember another song which flowed out more quickly. The group learned it at soundcheck, and we played it that evening. Over the years, so many people have related stories of how this song has helped them through difficult times. It is for the benefit of ourselves and others that the message in many Spirit songs has not diminished with the passage of time.

'Animal Zoo' (Ferguson) (3:11)

This longtime fan favorite rides in on the sounds of the city, accompanied by an infectious guitar riff that leads into Ferguson's soulful vocal. One by one, instruments are layered on top of California's guitars, until the entire band is rolling in the same direction. Ferguson's erudite lyric, speaks of alienation in the modern world – touching on environmental themes, framing it all quite cleverly:

Living in the city, I've been abused (He has)
The jobs I keep and people I meet
They don't do more than make me amused
Everywhere I turn now, just more bad news
So don't look now and don't ask how
Gonna find me a way to the animal zoo

The 'animal zoo' is some sort of hippie ideal – a back-to-the-country Eden that so many poets and rock songwriters dreamt of in the late-1960s and early-1970s.

'Love Has Found A Way' (California, Locke) (2:42)

This song is a tribute to the power of love and the eternal search for peace and brotherhood. California's lyric is filled with brilliant imagery:

31

Waves are crashing on the sea
Lens flashing on how it should be
Some are reaching for the gun
Some are searching for the sun

The memorable chorus is a statement of defiance in spite of the many
obstacles. Musically, this is one of Spirit's masterpieces, with carefully-crafted
layers concocted by producer Briggs and the band; a swirling psychedelic haze
bumping up against fascinating chimes and light percussion, while Randy's
guitars soar in the background.

'Why Can't I Be Free' (California) (1:05)
Jumping straight in with the slightest of pauses, this song serves as a sort of
coda to the previous song, bringing the concept of love to the romantic realm,
making it more personal: 'I don't know what it is to be free/And I cry when
you say that you can't free me (Please free me)/I just can't go on.' California's
elegant fretwork is accompanied by a melancholy vocal that – at the end –
floats away with the breeze.

'Mr. Skin' (Ferguson) (4:00)
Written in tribute to Ed Cassidy and his legendary bald pate, this muscular
rocker was destined to become a fan favorite. Aside from the song's sly groove
– fueled by Andes' spacey bass lines (He's been mostly inconspicuous up to
this point on the album) – there's Cassidy's spry percussion, Locke's keyboards
and odd sounds coaxed therefrom, and pointed guitar solos. It's the addition
of a funky horn break – the equal of any on a southern soul record – that leaves
its mark on 'Mr. Skin': taking the song out on a brassy note reminiscent of Sly
and the Family Stone.

'Space Child' (Locke) (3:25)
John Locke's songs on any Spirit album tend to be more cerebral fare, and
this is no different. An oddball instrumental, it starts out spacey and semi-
psychedelic, with rambling piano, echoed guitar that bounces from speaker
to speaker, and ominous bass. At some point, Locke breaks in with an eerie
synthesizer passage accompanied by a thick instrumental din. There's a bit
of jazz, rock, blues, and electronics swirling about in the mix, creating an
invigorating and enchanting instrumental soundscape. Randy's little guitar
flourishes on the fade-out are a nice touch, leading directly into …

'When I Touch You' (Ferguson) (5:37)
…the cataclysmic opening of 'When I Touch You': an instrumental tsunami
giving way to Randy's Jimi-jam guitar play. Ferguson's lofty vocal is at once
breathless and growling depending on the line, riding the backing track like a
bucking bronco. The lyric is a sort of acid poetry, appropriate for the backing:

'Often in my dreams/I see the strangest things/I see the mountains rise/I see them touch the skies'. California's stinging fretwork leaps from channel to channel, Cassidy's drums sound like a bulldozer, and Ferguson calls back to 'Why Can't I Be Free' with the final verse, singing, 'Your love holds all these keys/Why can't I be free from thoughts of bitter rage?,' while the music closes in around him like a hurricane. The result is an effective song with incredible instrumental performances.

'Street Worm' (Ferguson) (3:42)

Much of *Twelve Dreams* sees the band fusing a hard rock sound with their candy-colored jazz-flecked psych-blues roots. Nowhere is this more obvious than here. It's a muscular rocker with a simple but cutting lyric that chases 1960s-era thoughts of freedom:

I'll be happy flying on the rooftops
I'll be happy burning in the streets
I'll be happy moving when I wish to
I'll be happy saying how I please

Ferguson's enthusiastic vocal is punctuated by jagged guitar lines, melodic bass, discordant keyboard squalls and a steady rhythm that helicopters in beneath the high-flying instrumentation. California's most reckless lead = about two minutes in – is paired with Cassidy's Gatling-gun percussion and piano counterpoint.

'Life Has Just Begun' (California, 3:30)

An instrumentally-melancholy song that seems to have originated in some sort of fever dream, 'Life Has Just Begun' name-checks Kiowa – a mid-western American-Indian tribe known to be fierce warriors – and Odawa: a middle-America Indian tribe of traders. The lyric certainly doesn't shine much light on Randy's intention:

We walked in the dreams
And we knew it was married in the dreams
Strange as it seemed that we knew
Because life has just begun

Was Randy inventing some sort of creation myth? Beats me.

The music is not nearly as innovative as that of most of its predecessors, but from California's intricate six-string introduction and the mesmerizing guitar lines woven throughout to Ferguson's dreamlike vocal and Locke's cascading piano notes, there's beauty to be found. California said in the CD liner notes: 'This tune became a real group effort – everyone pitching in a piece of the puzzle, until, by *magic*, it was complete.'

'Morning Will Come' (California) (2:51)

Record labels are always carping at rock bands to write *hit singles* - even at the dawn of the 1970s with the emergence of FM radio as the predominant media format for teenage America. But when label execs are faced with a surefire radio hit – like 'Morning Will Come', let's say – they're a lock to choose a different song off the album to release on 45rpm and, when it stiffs on the charts, proclaim themselves correct, with collective pats on the back all around in recognition of their superior business savvy.

'Morning Will Come' was tailor-made for radio airplay, but never came anywhere near being released as a single. With a buoyant opening riff, group harmonies, pop-star vocals, scrappy horn-play and nonsensical lyrics that nevertheless say 'baby' and 'love' often enough to fool the marks, this up-tempo rocker had more than enough brightly-hued melody to hit the charts without scaring a single housewife into changing the station.

'Soldier' (California) (2:43)

Downright somnambulant compared to 'Morning Will Come', this psychedelic ballad nevertheless wields serious wizardry. The counterpoint vocal harmonies, the callback to previous songs on the album, the overall swirling, misty vibe and lush instrumentation all help make it a suitable sign-off to an incredible album that saw the band firing on all cylinders creatively. California said in the CD liner notes: 'For this track, David suggested we go to a special studio which had a real pipe organ. The majesty of this sound provided the perfect texture through which our heartfelt collective efforts could be summed up.'

Bonus Tracks:
'Rougher Road' (California) (3:16)

Bonus tracks on the CD reissues of Spirit's first four albums basically come in two flavors: songs good enough to have made the cut for the main album (a minority), and fair-to-middling songs not worthy of Spirit's collective genius (the majority of these bonus tracks): throwaways, better forgotten. 'Rougher Road' is a fine example of the former.

It's a song about life growing up in a rock-'n'-roll band. Matthew Greenwald of *AllMusic* summed it up best: 'Despite the simplicity of the song and the rough arrangement (It does sound like a well-rehearsed demo), there is a certain period charm here, especially in Randy California's fine vocal and guitar work.' It's hard to pick a spot on *Twelve Dreams* where you could easily slot 'Rougher Road' in, which shows how creative the band was during this period.

'Animal Zoo' (Mono single) (Ferguson) (3:10)

The mono version of the fan favorite: custom-designed for AM airplay. The stereo version still beats it hands-down.

'Morning Will Come' (Alternate mono mix) (California, 2:48)

Since this mono mix was created, it seems it was considered as a possible single. It's a shame because unlike much of the material on *Twelve Dreams*, 'Morning Will Come' loses little when shorn of its stereo effects, and the bright, electric performance would've sounded great on AM radio.

'Red Light Roll On' (California) (5:41)

The non-album B-side of 'Animal Zoo' is a fancy slab of booger rock that could've just as easily fit onto Jo Jo Gunne's debut album, even if California *did* write it. The verses sway back and forth from boogie blues to Spirit's trademark turf. But overall, it's a fine-sounding bit of fluff that really wasn't representative of *Twelve Dreams*.

The 2022 deluxe UK reissue of *Twelve Dreams* adds even more bonus tracks. Standouts include 'Dirty Dan' (a greasy Ferguson instrumental with blues hues and a funky swagger) and 'Walking On My Feet' (a California track best described as soft rock with a touch of psychedelic whimsy).

The reason to upgrade to this deluxe edition is for the previously-unreleased live disc featuring the original band performing at the Fillmore West in San Francisco on 16 May 1970. We're given a taste of the show at the end of disc one, with Randy's first live performance of 'Nature's Way' ('a song I wrote this afternoon'). The sixteen Fillmore tracks on disc two are a revelation, showcasing the band in its prime with an engaging setlist and fine performances. 'Mechanical World' was recorded in October 1969 at the Boston Tea Party venue in Boston, Massachusetts, and it's every bit as bombastic a performance as it should've been.

The sound quality is acceptable overall, though a little muddy at times, with some echo and an infrequent lack of instrumental separation. But try finding a live tape of the original band with better sonics.

Worldly Remains publisher Ron Garmon wrote of *Twelve Dreams* in his anthology *Lost In the Grooves*:

As Dr. Gonzo and the Brown Buffalo careened off the strip for Vegas, five guys from Topanga Canyon were putting the last touches on a concept-rock masterpiece on the death of the L.A. hippie dream. Doctor and attorney need not detain us further. Fuck 'em. Baking in the basin's hash and sunshine haze, was Spirit – a weld of heavy psych, fusion jazz and druggy mysticism, assembled out of a chance meeting during the 1967 Griffith Park love-ins ... after this elegant, uproarious, hard-rocking jazz-jumping funeral procession down Hollywood Blvd. for an OD'd hippie prince, Spirit disbanded. Accounts differ, but I think it was rock's first case of *Jesus, we can't top this!* No one has.

Feedback (1972)

Personnel:
John Christian Staehely (credited as Christian): guitar, vocals
Al Staehely: vocals, bass
John Locke: keyboards, synthesizer
Ed Cassidy: drums, percussion
Producer: David Briggs
Engineer: David Brown
Label: Epic Records
Release date: March 1972
Chart position: US: 63
CD reissue produced by Doug Wygal; remastered by Ken Robertson
Current edition: US: Collector's Choice Music, 2003 (CD); UK: Eastworld
Recordings, 2013 (CD)

The inter-group tensions that had first flared up during the recording of *Clear*, were channeled into a stream of unparalleled creativity by producer David Briggs on the *Twelve Dreams* album. But the volcano was about to blow, and after a short tour to promote *Twelve Dreams*, Spirit fractured, seemingly for good. California accused Ferguson and Andes of attempting to hijack the band, so they boogied off to the relatively mundane and ultimately short-lived Jo Jo Gunne in search of fame and fortune. In his 2001 interview with *Worldly Remains*, Ed Cassidy remembered: 'Jay was disillusioned with the fact that our band was not as big as we thought it should be. So I think his commercialism sort of boiled to the top. He thought he could get out there and get a good commercial rock-'n'-roll band and make history with that. I think that triggered a lot of the malfunction between Randy and Jay.'

Ferguson, unsurprisingly, has a slightly different view of his departure from Spirit. In his *Worldly Remains* interview, he said, 'I don't know how far back the thought of leaving took root. But I know Mark and I – as everybody in the band – we were all frustrated. Frustrated with business, frustrated with each other, frustrated with our girlfriends. So once again as you look at this album, it's sort of trying to get out. Trying to escape.' Of the aftermath of *Twelve Dreams*, Ferguson added, 'The synergy didn't hold after that. We flew apart. And I don't think we could've done another record: maybe in a couple of years.'

A musician named John Arliss originally took Andes' spot in the band, but when California hurt himself and was laid up for months, the remaining members John Locke and Ed Cassidy pondered Spirit's future. Ferguson introduced Locke to singer/bassist Al Staehely. Locke remembered in the liner notes of the 2003 *Feedback* CD reissue: 'We weren't even looking around. The first guy that walked through the door got the gig to be in Spirit.' Tour dates had already been booked, so they went out on the road as a three-piece. Locke said: 'There were a lot of people that wanted to hear the band. Our managers told promoters that this was a new lineup, and we did very well as a trio. It was pretty amazing. We played all over the East Coast and elsewhere.'

After the tour, it was time to record an album and fulfill the band's commitment to Epic Records. They recruited Al's younger brother John (a talented but green guitarist) from the Texas band Krackerjack, and went to work with producer Briggs at Columbia Records' Hollywood studios. The two Texans brought an entirely new musical direction to Spirit – a more-rootsy country-rock sound that eschewed the band's jazz and psych-rock tendencies. Released in early 1972, the band toured for the rest of the year. But as neither Locke nor Cassidy were particularly enamored of the new coat of paint afforded the Spirit sound, they soon left the band soon. The Staehelys finished up a European tour under the Spirit name with drummer Stu Perry, calling it quits in mid-1973 and recording an album for Epic titled *Sta-Hay-Lee*: credited to The Staehely Bros.

As for *Feedback*, it performed reasonably well, all things considered, matching the 63 chart position of *Twelve Dreams*. But *Feedback* went out of print somewhat quickly until Collectors' Choice Music reissued it on CD 30 years later: billing it as 'The long-lost 1972 album from Spirit.'

Critics were not very kind to the album. *Rolling Stone* critic John Mendelsohn wrote, referring to the Staehely brothers: 'if *Feedback* is an accurate indication of their talents, it's doubtful that these two new copilots will ever get the group back off the ground ... without trying to be snide, the only thing about this album that I find even minimally interesting, is its cover, which betrays roughly a trillion times more imagination than the music it encloses.'

Robert Christgau was a bit more charitable, awarding *Feedback* a 'B' grade, writing: 'In a way, Al Staehely's earthy rock and roll is a relief from the California spaces of what were supposedly this band's great days – songs as hard as his fast ones, aren't easy to come by these days.'

In *The History of Rock*, Max Bell referred to the Staehely brothers-led version of Spirit as 'this rather bogus outfit', concluding that *Feedback* was 'a collection with little to redeem it, and none of the magic of the earlier work.' In his *AllMusic* reappraisal, critic Joe Viglione is perhaps the most enthusiastic:

> Had the Staehely brothers and John Locke stayed on board for Cassidy and Randy California's next project, the erratic *Potatoland* disc may have mutated into something totally brilliant. The best of Al Staehely, John Locke and Randy California would have been truly something. *Feedback* is a solid performance and remarkable album, which deserves its place in the Spirit catalog, and not the status of bastard-son. It is a legitimate Spirit project, and it is very, very good.

In the July 2008 issue of *Shindig!*, editor Jon 'Mojo' Mills wrote that *Feedback* 'is a funny beast. Occasionally it sounds like Spirit ... elsewhere, the bluesy rock guitar persuasions and macho ruse of southern rock enters the frame. The ridiculously hippy sentiment of 'Mellow Morning', however, is a saving grace, with its cosmic-cowboy country emblems outdoing the workmanlike whiskey-laden swagger. Not a disaster by any means, but it ain't *Sardonicus* either.'

So, is *Feedback* a 'very, very good' album? The answer is complicated. It's a lousy Spirit album by any standard, in spite of the presence of Messrs. Locke and Cassidy. If it was by any other band of the period, rather than a growing cult-rock legend like Spirit, it would be judged differently, as maybe *mediocre* with moments of brilliance. As it stands today, it's an outlier in the Spirit catalog; the only album without Randy California. It remains a deservedly lost chapter in the band's history.

Interviewed by writer Mick Skidmore for *Shindig!* in 2009, John Locke commented on the *Feedback*-era version of Spirit: 'It's not a bad album, but again it wasn't Spirit. It's hard to say that anything that came out after the first four albums was anything but a side project or an attempt to recreate the past. That's the reality of it, including all Randy's efforts in later years, which, although was in name Spirit, they were really the Randy California Band – which is fine, because he did some great stuff.

'Chelsea Girls' (Staehely) (3:38)
I can see your average 1971 Spirit fan dropping the needle on *Feedback,* and hearing 'Chelsea Girls'. Al Staehely's southwest drawl is nowhere near Jay Ferguson's rock star vox, or even Randy California's hippie patois, and the song is needlessly gussied-up with female backing vocals and a rootsy honky-tonk arrangement more befitting Delaney & Bonnie and Friends than Spirit.

Brother John's guitar is given too few opportunities to shine, though his lead passage roughly two minutes in is quite biting, but Locke and Cassidy sound like different guys altogether. Al Staehely is a different sort of songwriter; a better lyricist than a singer:

> They say that Dylan Thomas drank himself to death
> But I know better
> It was them Chelsea girls that wouldn't give that boy no rest
> I said, 'Where are you Andy Warhol? Call your superstars off'
> It's been three days since food or sleep
> And I contracted a terrible cough, yes I did

It's a clever verse with hip counterculture references, untarnished by psychedelic frippery. But a song about getting some loving from the women in New York City, shouldn't sound like something you'd hear in an oil-riggers dive bar on the Texas Gulf Coast, should it?

'Cadillac Cowboys' (Staehely) (3:41)
If the opener 'Chelsea Girls' didn't tip off the anonymous Spirit fan imagined above that this was a different sort of band, then 'Cadillac Cowboys' provided

ample evidence that the new outfit was something more akin to the Staehely Brothers Blues Band. With Locke's vibrant juke-joint piano-pounding offering a melodic counterpoint to Brother Al's mugging, growling and grimacing vocals, the band boogie-woogies through the song with joyful, reckless abandon, which, as this song proves, doesn't always make for easy listening. It's a shame, as Staehely again delivers some observational and inspired lines about the masks people wear:

> Cadillac cowboys, you see 'em everywhere you go
> They ain't the ones that won the west
> They wear their spurs just for show

'Puesta del Scam' (Locke) (2:10)
This is more like it – an eclectic and electrifying instrumental performance that relies heavily on Locke's considerable keyboard skills, showcasing John Staehely's six-string abilities with a series of impressive solo passages, including some stereo-panning stunts. Cassidy sounds more engaged here, with subtle, percussive rhythms, and hints of Al Staehely's bass prowess rumble low in the mix, punctuating Locke's instrumental pyrotechnics.

'Ripe And Ready' (Staehely) (3:53)
Another boozy, bluesy construct, heavy on the Lone Star honky-tonk that the Staehely brothers cut their teeth on. This is a raunchy, lusty, less-than-wholesome love song that's long on attitude and short on anything resembling a radio-friendly melody or hook. Still, you've got to love lines like 'You be Juliet, I'm gonna be your Romeo/Curtain's up, let's start the show.' Locke's oddball keyboard passage comes out of left field, and John's solo shortly thereafter is too brief to be effective.

'Darkness' (Locke) (4:59)
Locke's piano intro slyly mixes classical notes with prog undertones; the music rising to a crescendo as the song takes a deft turn towards the sort of early-1970s art rock that bands like Saga or Triumvirat were then exploring. Locke turns in a decent-enough lyric that makes you wonder why he didn't write more:

> In the darkness of my time
> My friends are all losing their minds
> What is this place that we're living in
> Where laying back is called a sin?

Unfortunately, the female backing vocals turn an otherwise-impressive experiment with solid performances all around, into a badly-dated and overwrought attempt to gain radio airplay.

'Earth Shaker' (Staehely) (4:02)

Spirit gets down and funky with the gratuitous 'Earth Shaker' – a semi-boogie paint-by-numbers with a plodding track and an inane lyric about groupie love: 'Organ grinder, ain't hard to find her/Wink your eye and she's on the scene.' Brother John provides some imaginative and entertaining guitar licks on what is otherwise an unremarkable song – and the soulful backing vocalists are back, providing another layer to our onion of agony.

'Mellow Morning' (Staehely, Matt Andes) (2:30)

The country-ish 'Mellow Morning' is caught in the creative/commercial twilight zone between The First National Band, The Flying Burrito Brothers and Pure Prairie League.

It's a good song, actually, with a stream-of-consciousness lyric and a lively acoustic guitar. Staehely's vocal is more natural and less strained than on the harder material, and if he'd chosen this sort of laid-back pub rock direction for *Feedback*, the album might've won over some new fans in spite of the 180-degree turn in the band's sound and style.

'Right On Time' (Staehely) (2:50)

While not as countrified as its predecessor, this offers a similar hybrid of country twang and folkish lyricism. Even when the full band kicks in after verse one, there's still a carefully-crafted honky-tonk sound that works for the band. Staehely isn't trying to over-emote here, which means he's right in the sweet spot vocally, while Locke's Nashville-styled piano-pounding (R.I.P. Hargus 'Pig' Robbins) sounds like he was born and raised in Printer's Alley. Staehely's love lyric is also effective:

You came right on time
You gave my life a rhyme
A look in your eyes made me realize I was an empty man
I thought I couldn't love
Now I can

Staehely and the gang missed an opportunity with this country rock thing, as they did it as well as anybody in 1972 and better than most – easily achieving an earthy organic sound that British pub rock bands like Brinsley Schwarz, Unicorn or Help Yourself were pulling their hair out trying to replicate.

'Trancas Fog-Out' (Locke) (2:46)

This is one of Locke's more engaging and fast instrumentals. At less than three minutes in length, there's still plenty of space for each musician to get their licks in. Even if the mix is a bit busy and dominated by Locke's strident piano, in headphones, you can hear Al's jazz-like bass work, John's swirling six-string and Cassidy's fast rhythms.

'Witch' (Staehely) (5:25)

After three dynamic tracks in a row, *Feedback* ends with the rote 'Witch' – another boozy, bluesy, kitchen-sink rocker that uses all the old tricks in the worst ways. The lyric falls short of the literary Kerouac wordplay of earlier songs – 'She's all of eighteen/She's every young man's dream/She's so foxy'. An ignoble end to an otherwise unremarkable album.

Bonus track
'New York City' (Staehely) (3:37)

This appears on the 2003 *Feedback* CD reissue. And even if it's a Texas juke-joint jam not dissimilar to 'Witch') (but without the vocal histrionics), it could've replaced any song on the album. Musically it's somewhat mundane, and Staehely's real-life tale ventures into more lurid lyrics at times. But with repeated spins, it still holds up better than 'Witch' does.

Spirit of '76 (1975)

Personnel:
Randy California: vocals, guitar, bass
Barry Keene: bass, vocals
Ed Cassidy: drums, percussion
Additional Personnel:
Benji: Moog synthesizer, harpsichord
Producer: Randy California
Engineers: Blair Mooney, Craig Renton
Label: Mercury Records
Release date: May 1975
Chart position: US: 147
Current edition: UK: BGO Records, 2003 (CD)

Spirit of '76 launched the second stage of Spirit's career. They signed to Mercury Records, which was owned by Phonogram Inc.). The band was in reality, no more than Randy California and Ed Cassidy at this point. In the 2003 BGO Records CD reissue liner notes, Alan Robinson wrote: 'By the time of its recording, Spirit were a very different combo from that which cut four classic albums for the Epic Records label between 1968 and 1970. Only Ed Cassidy survived from the original lineup. Indeed, Randy California had only recently rejoined the band, having quit to pursue a short-lived solo career.' Robinson outlines California's travails in the wake of the failed 1981 *Kapt. Kopter* album: 'Moving to Molokai, Hawaii, California was destitute, living on the beach. Whilst there, he was taken in by a Christian family employing him as their gardener. Having found a level of moderate stability, he acquired a guitar, and started writing the songs that would form the basis of both *Spirit of '76* and its follow-up *Son Of Spirit.*'

California returned to the mainland, reunited with Cassidy and went about the business of getting the Spirit name back from Al Staehely, who retained possession of the band trademark by default after California had seemingly abandoned it.

Bringing bassist Mark Andes back into the fold, the trio toured the USA for six months circa 1974/1975; the material they performed forming the basis of *Spirit Of '76*. Taking advantage of an opportunity, the new Spirit took over a canceled Alvin Lee gig in Tampa, Florida, and promoted the show themselves, using the profits to record *Spirit Of '76*. Andes had drifted off to Firefall by this time, and California enlisted bassist/engineer Barry Keene to take his place, though Randy was to play most of the album's bass parts himself.

The sound and fury of the 1960s were hardwired into California's being by this time, and between his head injury and subsequent breakdown, he began a spiritual journey that's partially documented in *Spirit Of '76*. He'd become immersed in the teachings of the Urantia Foundation – a religious organization founded in the 1960s – and aspects of their spiritual philosophy is woven into the album's lyrics. It's also the first Spirit album on which Randy had complete creative control. As a musician and producer, he created a dreamy, stoned sound, drenched in phased and distorted guitars. Any of the songs might not stand alone, but taken as a whole, they form a brilliant tapestry of poetry and provocative sound.

Critics were nearly unanimous in overlooking *Spirit Of '76*, and *Creem* scribe 'Ranger Reek' Johnson seems to have been the only critic to have reviewed the album. Johnson, writing in the June 1976 issue, said, 'So now we're being asked to buy the '76 model of Spirit, with Randy, Ed and a bassist named Barry Keene. They're surprisingly listenable, considering. Although nowhere near the old band in style or power, they at least display a sense of humor which was sorely lacking in the last 20 regroupings.' Though Johnson's review leans positive, he concluded, 'Only fanatics need apply.'

Ed Cassidy discussed *Spirit of '76* in his 2001 *Worldly Remains* zine interview: 'I think it's a great album personally. I'll put the phones on and just listen to the whole thing from one end to another ... it stands the test of time as being a piece of music that will always be listenable, because it *is* listenable.' However, Cassidy was not nearly as enamored of the ersatz band's Mercury Records deal:

I didn't try to exert any influence on Randy in terms of contracts with the different record labels – which, in retrospect, hindsight, I probably should have. Whether they would have agreed to something else, I don't know. But the problem with Mercury and I.R.S. later on, is that Randy was doing a master purchase deal. They'd get the masters, and they'd give you so much money up front. End of story. Good luck ... you hope maybe you do something that's mind-boggling and startling enough, so it became super-famous. 'You want another one? It's gonna cost you.' ... we didn't get the promotion. Anyway, you go into that kind of thing with labels, and it's not uncommon. Mercury was one of those – and the same thing when we did *Son Of Spirit*. Anyway, all those independent deals from Randy, I never received anything really for those. It was difficult times with playing and performing. You had to take the good with the not so good.

The cover art was created by noted L.A. artist Burt Shonberg, who also co-wrote two spoken-word songs on *Spirit Of '76*. Shonberg was active from the late-1950s until his death in 1977, and was known for his grandiose murals, which adorned various L.A. coffee houses, nightclubs and restaurants. He also created cover art for albums by Arthur Lee & Love, The Curtis Brothers and The Modern Folk Quartet. His paintings appeared in movies like Roger Corman's *The Fall Of The House Of Usher,* and in 1958, he and his friend and business partner, novelist and screenwriter George Clayton Thomas opened a Laguna Beach coffee house called Café Frankenstein, for which Shonberg created unique signage. His paintings are hot stuff among Hollywood's glitterati, and highly collectible. You can find out more about Shonberg on the late artist's website at www.burtshonberg.com.

'America The Beautiful'/'The Times They Are A Changin''
(Katharine Lee Bates, Samuel A. Ward/Bob Dylan) (5:27)

What Hendrix did for 'The Star-Spangled Banner', Randy does with 'America The Beautiful' – giving the patriotic standard a low-key albeit hauntingly-beautiful performance. Though the song had been recorded by artists as diverse as Bing Crosby, Frank Sinatra and Ray Charles (who had a minor R&B-chart hit with it in 1976), nobody before or since delivered as heartfelt a performance as Randy.

The song starts with a bit of studio tomfoolery – an echoed spoken-word intro – and quickly segues into Randy's gorgeous acoustic picking and breathless vocals. The song moves seamlessly into Dylan's 'The Times They Are A Changin'', which fits perfectly – both songs given an intricate and elegant guitar line that expands the melody of each to completely transform both. Though there are still electronic artifacts in the background, they tend to complement what is a magnificent performance.

'Victim Of Society' (California, Cassidy) (3:00)

In contrast with the preceding song, this is a funky rocker with a socially-conscious lyric, a massive rhythmic backdrop and stellar fretwork. Randy's lyric tells of a child's difficult interaction with modern society and subsequent spiritual journey to find freedom: a common theme of his songs. The music is lush, multi-layered and exhilarating, with California taking the listener to one six-string crescendo after another, until the song's abrupt finish.

'Lady Of The Lakes' (California, Cassidy) (2:52)

Tentative in his attempts at singing, California found a middle ground between his usual soft-shoe vocal style and former Spirit frontman Jay Ferguson's pop-oriented approach. Randy began structuring songs for a talking-blues style delivery – as he does here – allowing for a sort of melodic spoken-word that pushes the theme across without detracting too much from the rich instrumentation. Somewhere in the middle, another voice chimes in scatting (Cassidy?), as a sort of counterpoint that adds to the song's overall energy.

'Tampa Jam (Pt. 1)' (California, Cassidy) (0:54)

The first of three short, sharp jams, this revisits the psychedelic era, with wafting vocals and guitar noodling that segues directly into…

'Maunaloa' (California) (2:02)

Inspired by Randy's time in Hawaii, 'Maunaloa' is a wistful ode to the rural village on the island of Molokai. With joyful lyrics, up-tempo music and vocal harmonies, the song rambles on to an odd instrumental fade-out, seemingly at odds with the song's *joie de vivre*.

'What Do I Have?' (California) (2:04)

An introspective ballad dominated by sparse fretwork and a rumbling bass. Randy kind of meanders all over the place here lyrically, as he frames his spiritual journey with the ethereal sound of his guitar and voice floating in tandem.

'Sunrise' (California, Cassidy) (3:00)

An unabashed hard rocker, with Cassidy's explosive drumming front-and-center in the mix. California's voice is all but lost in a cacophony of guitars and jagged bass licks.

'Walking The Dog' (Rufus Thomas) (3:13)

Revisiting the 1963 Memphis soul classic by Stax Records legend Rufus Thomas (which California recorded again for his 1981 solo LP *Kapt. Kopter*), Randy throws in a few more studio effects for good measure, but otherwise delivers a high-flying and funky take, with a little more chaotic over-the-top guitar than previously. Otherwise, it's a serviceable cover with a swaggering vocal and an infectious, reckless vibe.

'Tampa Jam (Pt. 2)' (California, Cassidy) (1:03)

The second 'Tampa Jam' is slightly longer, but even wiggier – California calling on his inner Jimi to deliver a psychedelic interlude.

'Joker On The Run' (California, Cassidy, Keene) (3:53)

Brief studio chatter leads into this country-flavored song – a refreshing change of pace from the album's hippie daze. Cassidy's big beats lead into a raucous guitar solo that takes the song from Flying Burrito Brothers territory to an unexpected hairy-chested arena rock sound, circling back again between the two extremes, before finally ending like a shitkickin' Poco track with Randy's fancy chicken-pickin'.

'When?' (California) (4:27)

Cassidy's bombastic percussion opens with an exotic Latin-esque rhythm, before slowing down to a crawl as California's outer-space guitar notes float in alongside his lofty vocal. The words are all but indecipherable (chasing after spiritual fulfillment, I'd guess), but the music is hypnotic and soothing: like a hot bath with an LSD chaser.

'Like A Rolling Stone' (Bob Dylan) (8:54)

When in doubt, dig into the Bob Dylan songbook, and few artists would bring as unique a vision to The Scribe's music as would Randy California. Picking back up on the acoustic guitar sound he used for 'The Times They Are A-Changin'', California expands it with an even more dazzling, disorienting, psych-drenched improvisation. Though his vocal starts as mere gossamer threads lost in the shadow of the swirling guitars and chanting percussion, Randy suddenly bursts into full voice roughly halfway through – increasing the lyric's impact as the music swells towards a totally enchanting finish, with hints of harpsichord floating in on the edge to offer an alternative to the guitar-heavy performance. The multitracked guitars are simply stunning, with a few studio effects added, but otherwise innately organic and exceptional in their execution.

'Once Again' (California, Cassidy) (3:19)

With Space Invaders video game-styled electronic squeals balanced by Cassidy's deep drum rhythms, 'Once Again' develops into an oddball rocker with random sound effects (an alarm clock keeps chiming in the background). The words are mostly delivered machine-gun style or are barely there, concealed behind layers of shimmering guitars. Randy's ability to multitrack the album's disparate instrumental performances into carefully-crafted soundscapes might've pointed towards a successful career in production, but I guess that his muse demanded a more performative expression.

'Feeling In Time' (California, Cassidy) (3:27)

Not quite a ballad, but not really a rocker, this seems to fall into that Laurel Canyon/Avocado Mafia singer-songwriter style defined by talents like Jackson Browne, J. D. Souther and Joni Mitchell in the early-1970s. Featuring one of Randy's more expressive vocal performances, his wan voice slots in alongside the jazz-like guitar licks and bass counterpoint. Cassidy's subtle rhythm work is supportive, and the song fades out with tasteful keyboard and cowbell. Without a strong enough presence to have played well on radio, 'Feeling In Time' is nevertheless one of California's most engaging performances.

'Happy' (Mick Jagger, Keith Richards) (3:19)

This Rolling Stones' hit from their 1972 *Exile On Main Street* album has been covered live and on record by performers as varied as Nils Lofgren, The Pointer Sisters, The Replacements, Lucinda Williams and Southside Johnny and The Asbury Jukes. Needless to say, Spirit's version is radically different – California and Cassidy keeping the song's underlying melody and throwing everything else into the bin. Instead, they substitute sharp-pointed guitar licks, droning vocals hidden beneath the mix, and layers upon layers of dense instrumentation, including thunderstorm rhythms, transforming the song into a truly joyous celebration.

'Jack Bond' (Burt Shonberg) (1:39)

This spoken-word piece is the album's cover-art designer Burt Shonberg performing as his Jack Bond alter-ego. It's an album outlier but somehow still works. His rambling voice is slightly electronically altered by various psychedelic effects until the song explodes under the weight of its own preposterousness.

'My Road' (California) (4:13)

A lovely mid-tempo rocker with squalls of instrumentation nearly burying the vocals, the semi-biographical 'My Road' offers California's winsome vocals, a mournful lyric and a brightly-colored palette of swirling guitars. The song rises and ebbs like the Pacific tides, with multi-hued fretwork and what's probably Cassidy's most nuanced and decorative rhythmic performance to date. Throw in judicious use of harmonica, and counterpoint vocals that mimic those from *Twelve Dreams*, and you have a truly spectacular performance.

'Tampa Jam (Pt. 3)' (California, Cassidy) (0:54)

This closes the trilogy with chattering drums and cowbell, California repeatedly chanting 'Tampa Jam', and barely-there guitars fading in and out of existence.

'Thank You Lord' (California) (1:45)

Randy California doesn't get nearly the acclaim he should for his production acumen, which comes into full force here. A simple spiritual that opens with doppler wave-sounding flanged guitar and vocal lines from 'The Times They Are A Changin'', the song is quickly clad in gospel garb, with California's reverent vocal, and hymnal piano work.

'Urantia' (California, Cassidy) (4:04)

Soaring again into the outer reaches of space, 'Urantia' is an atypical psychedelic construct, relying on a handful of electronic effects that are paired with Cassidy's rolling 'Caravan'-styled drums and Randy's squonky fretwork. It's a pleasant interlude, but slotted here between the gospel of 'Thank You Lord' and the jazz-flecked 'Guide Me', it's a bit out of place.

'Guide Me' (California, Cassidy) (3:47)

A truly *out-there* track that's mostly instrumental (the vocal doesn't kick in until around 2:25), the song starts with the sound of a crowd, possibly at a party, as Randy's jazzy guitar part rambles in along with Cassidy's imaginative percussion. The song slowly grows into a mellow, latin-rock construct until fading out around 1:45 and fading back in with what appears to be the sound of a couple of jabrones playing ping-pong. The six-string returns, then there's rapid percussion as the volume grows and the song finishes in a flurry of noise and chaos. Not the best performance on the album, but possibly the most interesting.

'Veruska' (California, Cassidy, Mark Andes) (3:57)

Since I wrote about an earlier version of the song as a bonus track on the *Spirit* CD, I'm going to let critic and Spirit fan Matthew Greenwald take this one. Writing for *AllMusic*, he says, 'Starting off with a tasty folksy, almost classical guitar figure from Randy California, 'Veruska' quickly mutates into a hard rock tribute to Wes Montgomery. On this track, Spirit's excellent jazz chops are in full evidence, as is their fine ensemble playing.' He's not kidding – this version is electrifying.

'Hey Joe' (Billy Roberts) (6:30)

Randy revisited Billy Roberts' garage-rock classic time-and-time-again over his career – certainly learning the song at the feet of his mentor Jimi Hendrix, who famously scored a top-10 UK hit with it in 1967. Randy adds a few instrumental flourishes of his own, and if his vocal isn't as inherently menacing as Hendrix's original reading, Randy's quivering, shimmering switchblade guitar solos take the performance to an entirely different dimension altogether.

'Hey Joe' has a history deserving its own book. Credited to California-based folk songwriter Billy Roberts – who copyrighted the song in 1962 – the sordid tale of a man on the run to Mexico after killing his cheating wife was allegedly based on the traditional 20th-century ballad 'Little Sadie,' but was also said to have been influenced by the song 'Baby, Please Don't Go To Town', by Roberts' former girlfriend Niela Horn, and by songwriter Boudleaux Bryant's 'Hey Joe!' (a 1952 hit by country star Carl Smith). Also, Scottish folk singer Len Partridge claimed he helped Roberts write the song in the 1950s. Further confusing the issue, Roberts' friend Dino Valenti (later of Quicksilver Messenger Service) had been performing the song and registered a copyright in his own name. Regardless of its origin, 'Hey Joe' has been recorded hundreds of times by a veritable who's-who of rock, folk and R&B artists – including The Leaves (who scored a minor chart hit with it in 1966), Tim Rose, The Standells, Love, The Music Machine, The Byrds, Cher, Wilson Pickett, Willy DeVille, Deep Purple and Roy Buchanan.

'Jack Bond (Pt. 2)' (Shonberg) (0:51)

'Jack Bond' returns for a coda of sorts, Randy heavily altering Shonberg's spoken words with echo and EQ-filtering, so they seep into your brain by osmosis, to the point that you're questioning your sanity.

'The Star-Spangled Banner' (Francis Scott Key, John Stafford Smith) (3:40)

Jimi Hendrix reclaimed the national anthem for the youth of America with his dazzling performance at the Woodstock Festival in 1969; his incendiary take layering a new coat of purple haze onto the moldy traditional dirge. The performance obviously had an effect on Randy, and here the young guitarist straps on his mentor's influence and takes the song entirely into left field.

After an Ed Sullivan-style introduction ('Now ladies and gentlemen, the Spirit of '76'), Randy delivers the lyric in a slight monotone above a shuffling rhythm with Cassidy's exotic bongo-beating in the background. The performance stands in stark contrast to Hendrix's Woodstock performance – California instead infusing the song with intricate guitar patterns, percussive flourishes and a miasma of instrumentation until he sticks the landing with a Sousa-approved outro, closing the song and the album.

Son Of Spirit (1975)

Personnel:
Randy California: vocals, guitar, bass
Barry Keene: bass, vocals
Ed Cassidy: drums, percussion
Producer: Randy California
Engineers: Blair Mooney, Barry Keene, Gary Brandt, Steve Mantoani, Keith Olsen
Label: Mercury Records
Release date: October 1975
Chart position: Did not chart
Current edition: UK: BGO Records, 2004 (CD)

Spirit's second Mercury Records album is a hodgepodge of stylistic experimentation and pop architecture. Comprised largely of songs that didn't make the last album, and some written much earlier, *Son Of Spirit* is largely a Randy California solo album constructed from demos and loose ends. The overall sound quality is decent but uneven, and he could've used an outside producer to temper his more colorful tendencies. Though the album could've used a little more gloss to liven up some songs for FM radio, taken altogether, *Son Of Spirit* is a remarkable feat, and save for a couple of hiccups, shows the 24-year-old's fairly deft hand and a modest evolution in his songwriting and production skills. Ed Cassidy's presence is sorely missed on several songs – his role on those occupied by a drum machine providing perfunctory rhythms. But California's uncanny ability to weave multiple vocal and instrumental tracks into a coherent, creative and entertaining record is astounding.

In his liner notes for the album's 2004 CD reissue, Alan Robinson sums up the album perfectly, writing, '*Son Of Spirit* was more recorded evidence of the rejuvenation of California's muse, and showed Spirit as a creative, contemporary rock combo far from trading on past glories.' Sadly, the critics were now largely ignoring Spirit, and there were few reviews of the album. Later reassessing it for *AllMusic*, Joe Viglione was enthusiastic:

> As *Spirit Of '76* is one of this pared-down band's most satisfying gambles, *Son Of Spirit* brings it together. It's the kind of chapter to the story, that Ian Anderson would develop for Jethro Tull: very musical, and shying from the commercial side of things. Definitely for the fans and for those hardcore Spirit fans who are out there, the acoustics and precise vocals are a treat … this album is refreshingly new, exciting, and a direction that deserved far more attention than it received.

The album was recorded at a number of studios, including Studio 70, Sound City, Wally Heider's, Larrabee Sound and the Record Plant. Interestingly, one of the engineers was Keith Olsen. An aspiring bass player, Olsen made his bones as a member of 1960s band The Music Machine: which enjoyed a top-

20 hit with 'Talk Talk' in 1966. Olsen later collaborated with The Millennium's genius songwriter/producer Curt Boettcher, and went on to engineer albums by The James Gang, Emitt Rhodes, Dr. John, and the promising young duo Buckingham Nicks. Olsen introduced Lindsey Buckingham and Stevie Nicks to Mick Fleetwood; later producing the new Fleetwood Mac's self-titled and chart-topping 1975 album. Olsen subsequently produced Grateful Dead, Eddie Money, Heart, Joe Walsh, Journey, Foreigner, Scorpions and many others – a veritable Murderer's Row 1970s/1980s rock stars – on his way to earning 39 Gold, 24 Platinum, and 14 Multi-Platinum album certifications. It's a shame he didn't work further with Randy California.

'Holy Man' (California) (2:55)
Opening with a rambling acoustic guitar pattern inspired by slack-key guitar that Randy heard in Hawaii, his soft, slightly-phased vocal rolls out his erudite, soul-seeking lyric. It's a simple song, augmented with studio effects and light congas; its lofty, jazzy air taking the guitarist's penchant for psychedelia in a refreshing new direction. In the 2004 reissue liner notes, California says, 'The Holy Men throughout human history have all had the same message. Every human being is given the opportunity to convey those divine qualities of fairness and compassion.'

'Looking Into Darkness' (California, Cassidy) (2:57)
Cut from the same lyrical cloth as its predecessor, this song writes another chapter in California's spiritual journey. While the vocal is unremarkable – though effective – it's the accompaniment that stands out. Layering guitars and vocals a mile high, and piling on the electronics, points to a new musical direction for his wandering attention. With Cassidy not around or unavailable, it's too bad about the generic pseudo-disco drum-machine rhythm. But the subtle, multitracked fretwork imbues the performance with a certain elegance.

'Maybe You'll Find' (California) (2:36)
Things sure go south quickly after the high points (and expectations) of the opening songs. 'Maybe You'll Find' is the first song here sounding like a demo – Randy's half-formed vocal accompanied by wishy-washy strings and an overall wimpy arrangement. As close to the dreaded Adult Contemporary radio format as anything Spirit has ever recorded, Randy's otherwise heartfelt and clever lyric was lost in the dreck in the attempt to record a hit. It's a shame, because the song has some lovely verses:

I think that if you sing a million songs
None of them would really turn you on
But the one thing that I know
When you open up your door
One note's enough in more than any song

The track is a textbook example of why artists often need a producer to bounce ideas off and help shape the songs.

'Don't Go Away' (California) (3:43)

This more-concise distillation of musical ideas, opens with a lengthy instrumental comprised of Randy's kitchen-sink studio process. High, lonesome guitar parts ride the tide as various sounds echo. Randy's vocal is electronically enhanced to match the gorgeous guitar lines: the overall effect being that of a joyous ode to love and romance.

'Family' (California) (3:08)

This is perhaps the album's most adventurous song. The exotic rhythm that opens this up-tempo semi-rocker was written three years previously. California's vocal takes a wild ride through his many expressions – from his normal, breathless delivery, to soaring verses and even a joyfully-reckless falsetto that recalls Queen's Roger Taylor. Against an unusual and jaunty backdrop, California's risk pays off with a strangely melodic and effective performance befitting the Spirit name. With a little polish to make it more radio-friendly, 'Family' could've been an interesting single.

'Magic Fairy Princess' (California) (2:57)

This is another exhilarating performance. With a strong melodic hook, imaginative fantasy lyrics, lush and creative instrumentation and dollops of gorgeous guitar, Randy made some true magic with another romantic effort as bold and bright as 'Maybe You'll Find' was dull and predictable. He hits a few bum notes as he reaches for the heavens, but that's all part of the song's charm.

'Circle' (California) (3:28)

Opening with an intricate and slight Piedmont blues guitar texture, other instruments slowly slide into the groove with the multitracked guitars. Yet another fine romantic tune, Randy's blues roots shine in his muted harmonica-playing and subtle guitar lines, while guitars glimmer from like the first rays of the new rising sun. With four top-notch love songs in a row offering varied degrees of nuance and emotion, California has found a niche I wish he'd explored more. Reminiscent of late-1960s Beatles and Rolling Stones, Randy manages to blend British Invasion melody with 1970s Southern California cool.

'The Other Song' (California, Cassidy, Keene) (5:41)

The album's only song credited to Spirit as a band, pairs an economic Cassidy rhythm with trippy space-ace guitar pyrotechnics. The song breaks down into a jazz swing about three minutes in – Randy pulling off his best George Benson imitation. The lyric is nothing to write home about, somewhat trite and repetitive – 'I was sneaking down, sneaking down, sneaking down the long lonesome road/But you were sleeping in your sad, precious smile' – but California sells them with a strong and uncharacteristic, brassy vocal.

'Yesterday' (John Lennon, Paul McCartney) (1:58)
California was no stranger to The Beatles' immense songbook, and he dives in and pulls out a plum with this gorgeous cover. Against a miasma of swirling sound, he perfectly captures the song's nostalgic melancholy with a wistful vocal and a filigree of multitracked guitars.

'It's Time Now' (California, 3:00)
A mid-tempo pop tune that was initially conceived for the *Potatoland* project (more about which later), this rose-colored lyrics sound inane until heard in the context of the shelved project, where they sound right at home. It's only slightly melodic, but is mesmerizing nevertheless, with ringing acoustic tones playing off sharper electric guitar notes, bells and chimes and some vocal harmonies. It's another joyful moment on an album where – with his unfettered muse allowed to play freely – California sounds like he's having the time of his life.

Farther Along (1976)

Personnel:
Randy California: vocals, guitar
Matt Andes: guitar, vocals
Mark Andes: bass, vocals
John Locke: keyboards
Ed Cassidy: drums, percussion
Additional personnel:
Ernie Watts: tenor saxophone ('Stoney Night')
Michael D. Temple: mandolin ('Don't Lock Up Your Door')
Steve Larrance: percussion
Ian Underwood: lead coconut ('Pineapple')
David Blumberg, Nick DeCaro: string and horn arrangement
Don Hederson: orchestration
Producer: Al Schmitt
Engineers: Mark Piscitelli, Bob Hughes, Jay Kauffman, Alan Sides
Label: Mercury Records
Release date: June 1976
Chart position: US: 179
Current edition: UK: BGO Records, 2004 (CD)

Farther Along represented a *de facto* reunion of the original band, sans vocalist Jay Ferguson, who by 1976 had launched a moderately successful solo career that was to carry him to the decade's end.

Bringing back stalwarts Mark Andes and John Locke, and adding Mark's brother Matt as second guitarist, California took advantage of the full band ensemble to pursue a lively, if downright-schizophrenic grab-bag of different musical styles.

In the album's 2004 CD-reissue liner notes, Alan Robinson waxes enthusiastic about the reunion effort:

Whether the near-reformation was intended to be anything other than a temporary move on California's part, is unclear. But what was immediately apparent – then and now – is how seamlessly California's creativity adjusted to the reorientation ... *Farther Along* is little short of superb – a splendid reaffirmation of the Spirit sound ... another significant step in California's artistic rehabilitation from his earlier breakdown.

I'm afraid I have to disagree. A full quarter of the album pursues a second-rate disco sound suspiciously designed to attract AM radio airplay. Only three songs here approach anything sounding even remotely like 1976 rock music. The rest are teeming with cheesy and overbearing strings and woodwinds that were somebody's idea of classy but which failed to elevate the material above the mundane.

53

How much of *Farther Along* was influenced by Al Schmitt is unknown, but the award-winning engineer and producer had a stellar track record to this point, producing classic albums by Jefferson Airplane and Jackson Browne, among others. Say what you will about *Feedback*, but at least the Staehely Brothers had a unique vision and pursued it. The artistic weaknesses of *Farther Along* are only magnified by the album's overall chamber-music vibe. In a year where rock albums by heavy-hitters like Lynryd Skynyrd, Thin Lizzy, Blue Öyster Cult, Boston, Bob Seger and Peter Frampton sold by the truckload while blowing up FM radio playlists, *Farther Along* falls short of hitting the mark by a mile.

Though critics largely ignored *Farther Along* when it was released, critical reassessment has been strangely sympathetic. Writing for *AllMusic*, Joe Viglione says the album 'has some very special moments,' and, aside from 'Atomic Boogie,' is 'an otherwise excellent album,' and that Spirit was a 'unique and important rock group.' Interestingly, while much of *Farther Along* was included as part of *The Mercury Years* compilation, that set included overdubs that were not part of the original recordings – an oversight corrected by BGO Records, who used the original mixes for their CD reissue.

'Farther Along' (California, Cassidy, Mark Andes) (3:21)

Remember that confused Spirit fan from a few chapters back, listening to *Feedback* for the first time and wondering, 'What the hell?' Well, *Farther Along* would have likely blown his/her mind. The title-track opener begins promisingly enough, with a plaintive vocal riding the currents above a string-laden arrangement peppered with acoustic guitar. Then it gets kind of twangy, like cut-rate Firefall, before meandering off into a dreamlike sonic horizon. It's not a bad song, but unexpected, with Matt Andes adding interesting rhythm guitar beneath Randy's scattershot psychedelic wanderings.

'Atomic Boogie' (California, Cassidy, Locke, Mark Andes, Matt Andes) (2:40)

If 'Farther Along' had the listener scratching their head in wonder, then 'Atomic Boogie' might just prompt them to turn off the record player and run off to join a monastery. With a funky, pseudo-disco rhythm, the track bull-rushes its way into your eardrums with total reckless disregard for the band's musical history. It's a failed attempt at funking up the Spirit sound – the fusion of Earth, Wind & Fire and KC and the Sunshine Band, poorly executed and failing miserably.

'World Eat World Dog' (California, Locke, Cassidy) (2:45)

Opening with a bossa nova rhythm on what is otherwise a decent enough Spirit song offering some interesting lines ('Each time you take a fall/It's a world eat world dog') above Randy's sparse guitar licks and Locke's piano flourishes. Musically, it's a treacly mess, with simpering strings dominating the instrumentation. Whether it was David Blumberg or Nick DeCaro that added the strings, they're certainly not in the league of Marty Paich, who displayed a lighter hand on Spirit's early LPs.

'Stoney Night' (California) (2:31)
The third disaster in a row, with Ernie Watts' blaring, out-of-place saxophone forever marring whatever Randy was trying to accomplish. I hear the lyrics in my head as part of a traditional hard-rocking Spirit song ('Call it wild like a circus child, and live for the day'), but the sad attempt to be radio-friendly, sullies the good Spirit name.

'Pineapple' (Locke, 2:12)
John Locke's obligatory instrumental track is a curious addition, sequenced as it is after a trio of horrible disco tunes. With a spry piano line and syncopated percussion, it's a lively and charming jaunt across an exotic musical landscape made all the more interesting by the coconut-bongo sound contributed by former Mothers of Invention multi-instrumentalist and musical MVP Ian Underwood.

'Colossus' (California, 2:57)
Six songs into *Farther Along*, the real Spirit emerges with a mid-tempo rocker that nevertheless sports a lush, busy instrumental soundtrack behind Randy's soft-spoken vocals and nimble acoustic guitar picking. Not the best of Spirit songs, but a welcome respite from the AM radio fodder that preceded it (extra credit for the return of the Ed Cassidy's 'big beat' and Locke's miasma of keyboard effects). Randy rips off a mighty impressive songwriting effort, with this poetic verse especially standing out:

> Where're you going, with that suitcase in your hand,
> Going to preach the gospel throughout the land.
> You're just on the road to oblivion,
> Can't you tell when your work is done?

'Mega Star' (California, Locke, 3:27)
Every one of Spirit's Mercury-era albums has an experimental song that stands out as a potential expansion of the band's sonic palette. 'Mega Star' is that song on *Farther Along*, the performance dominated by Locke's raging piano-pounding, which welds classical outlines with more avant-garde sounds, like Keith Jarrett mixed with, well, Ian Underwood's MOI-era keyboard flights of fancy. Randy's voice is in fine form, and his guitar meshes well with Locke's burnished ivories, while the rest of the band just hangs on for dear life, adding what they can to the mix.

'Phoebe' (Andes, 2:10)
Matt Andes is provided a spotlight here for his not-inconsiderable talents, this gorgeous instrumental benefitting from a sympathetic arrangement and fine

production work. The sound of the guitars flows like sunlight glinting off a wave kissing the beach and while it's a bit over-orchestrated for my taste, it's nevertheless a beautiful performance.

'Don't Lock Up Your Door' (California, Cassidy, Mark Andes, 3:10)

Spirit gets 'back to the country' with a bluesy, rootsy tune that crosses Canned Heat with Poco and gets good results. Michael Temple's electrifying mandolin play adds a lot to the song, with Randy's fleet acoustic licks offering a valuable counter-balance to the reedier-sounding mandolin strum; Andes and Cassidy deliver a bedrock rhythmic backdrop; and California's vocals are just lofty enough to pull it all together into an enjoyable performance. I would have liked to hear more of this and less of 'Stoney Night' on *Farther Along*, and while Spirit long flirted with a countryish sound, they never bought into the change 100% (as they probably should have, given that roots-rock was mid-1970s chic).

'Once With You' (California, Locke, 1:33)

Another heavily-orchestrated 'Adult Contemporary' track from a band musically unable to settle for such dreck, 'Once With You' is thankfully incredibly short and annoying, making one wonder how it made the cut for the final tracklist, to begin with.

'Diamond Spirit' (California, Mark Andes, 2:25)

There's a germ of a decent Spirit song here in 'Diamond Spirit', with forceful vocals from Randy, strident guitar strum, and a fierce underlying rhythm ... all of which is totally muddied and muddled beneath an avalanche of horribly weeping strings.

'Nature's Way' (California, 2:04)

I normally don't like symphonic incursions into the world of rock 'n' roll, but there are exceptions. The Moody Blues' *Days Of Future Past* is a good example of classical/rock fusion, as is Rick Wakeman's *Journey To The Center of the Earth*. Proggers like Emerson, Lake & Palmer, Greenslade, and even early Electric Light Orchestra did some cool things mixing musty old sounds with new ideas, so this wasn't exactly an alien landscape for Spirit to venture across at the time. This orchestral, instrumental re-imagining of the band's classic 'Nature's Way' works precisely because of the song's familiarity with fans and its strong underlying melody, which is amplified by the symphonic interpretation. I wouldn't want a steady diet of this sort of thing, but it's a pleasant enough way to finish up an otherwise disappointing album.

Future Games (A Magical-Kahauna Dream) (1977)

Personnel:
Randy California: vocals, guitar, bass
Ed Cassidy: drums, percussion
Additional personnel:
Terry Anderson: vocals
Jon Kotleba: synthesizer
Producer: Randy California
Engineers: Blair Mooney, Randy California
Label: Mercury Records
Release date: April 1977
Chart position: Did not chart
Current edition: UK: BGO Records, 2005 (CD)

After the ill-fated Spirit reunion that resulted in the ramshackle *Farther Along*, California still owed Mercury Records another album, which he delivered in the form of *Future Games: A Magical-Kahauna Dream*. Assembled from solo recordings and studio experimentation, the album is a maddening, meandering collection of good ideas half-realized, with strong instrumental performances from California and Cassidy but no real sense of direction outside of Randy's internal monologue.

For all of his studio acumen, Randy California was prone to creative excesses. Although a wizard at capturing the sounds that were rattling around in his head, by self-producing albums like *Future Games* and *Son Of Spirit* without another pair of ears to judge his ideas, California robbed the band of any sort of commercial potential. Without a voice of authority to say 'no' every now and then, however, California's id often ran amok across the grooves.

Which isn't to say that *Future Games* isn't an entertaining and engaging recording. California crafted a sly collection of pop/rock material that, sadly, failed as effortlessly as its Mercury label predecessors. Although he samples dialogue (too) freely from *Star Trek* as well as other television shows and movies (an artistic choice that was as groundbreaking as it was audacious), the proof is in the grooves and many of the songs here are among the best of California's creations during the Mercury Records era. Still, given the feeble chart showing of Spirit's previous three albums for the label, I'm surprised that they actually released this somewhat self-indulgent recording with grandiose musical aspirations.

Needless to say, Spirit was old news to critics in 1977, and they ignored *Future Games* in favor of shiny new recordings from contemporary bands. Still, in a year that included albums like Television's *Marquee Moon*, Todd Rundgren & Utopia's *Ra*, The Residents' *Fingerprince*, and Brand X's *Moroccan Roll* as well as punk rock debuts from The Clash, The Ramones, Buzzcocks, The Damned, and The Saints, was *Future Games* really that far outside of the zeitgeist?

Modern critics have been much kinder to *Future Games* in reassessing the album for the new millennium. In *The Guardian* newspaper in 2013, Paul Lester wrote that the album 'couldn't have been more bright and buoyant. Weird, for sure, but hardly depressing'. In revisiting the album, Lester correctly places it at the center of pop culture circa 1977:

> In a way, *Future Games* was the first collage-pop album, made out of samples: television and movie dialogue and assorted pop culture detritus, four years before Byrne and Eno's *My Life In The Bush of Ghosts*. Maybe the world wasn't ready for California's latest crazed scheme; although released as it was in early 1977, it now seems incredibly punk. Trippy yet terse ... it was as though California was applying the aesthetic and cartoon logic of The Ramones to the spaced-out freakiness of The Grateful Dead.

In his review of Spirit's *Sunrise and Salvation* box set for *Ugly Things* magazine, Steve Krakow (a/k/a 'Plastic Crimewave') writes of *Future Games*, 'seriously folks, this is one of the most beautifully demented albums I've ever encountered, and just so far ahead of its time the world has yet to realize or catch up to its friendly brilliance'.

'CB Talk' (California, 0:42)
Opening the album with a satire of America's mid-1970s CB (Citizen's Band) Radio craze doesn't provide a particularly auspicious beginning for *Future Games*, but here we are. With a far-away radio playing a native Hawaiian song in the background, Randy swaps 'CB talk' with another 'trucker' and hypes the new album. Advertising man and part-time country singer C.W. McCall (née William Dale Fries, Jr.) scored a monster hit a year earlier with the CB-themed song 'Convoy', which sold an astounding two million singles and spawned a hit movie starring Kris Kristofferson and Ali MacGraw. Maybe Randy was hoping a little of that CB mania would help sell *Future Games*, I dunno...

'Stars Are Love' (California, 2:29)
'CB Talk' segues into and overtop of the intro to 'Stars Are Love', a typical entry in California's 1970s-era spiritual songs. He's going for a different sort of sound here, and Jon Kotleba's synthesizer buzzes and hums like a swarm of angry bees while Randy's lovely spoken-song vocals ride along on waves of dazzling acoustic guitars. The lyrics are pretty nifty, too – 'Bad luck and trouble will meet you, when all the stars will greet you, if you set the world on fire, your heart is made of desire' – and the busy background helps create an exhilarating effect.

'Kahauna Dream' (California, 2:44)
Inspired by his time in Hawaii, 'Kahauna Dream' is similar in Spirit to Randy's earlier song, 'Maunaloa'. Backed by a vaguely exotic rhythm (mildly Martin

Denny-ish), California embroiders the song with wiry and diverging guitar lines. Although he muddies up the mix with found sounds and studio stuff, Randy's lyrics here are imaginative: 'just riding on a crystal chime that I feel I still can ride, you gave me the key and I open the door, love is all there is no more'. It's a trippy song with a romantic message and an infectious island vibe.

'Buried In My Brain' (California, Kim Fowley, Blair Mooney, Carla Savage, 2:55)

Displaying a little harder edge than his material has in years, 'Buried In My Brain' is a gang-written effort, although lyrics like 'the food you used to eat doesn't taste the same, kinda space you can't control, losing your grip on pain, living in a soundless dream, nothing is ever real' seem like vintage Randy to these ears. Electric guitars roar like hungry beasts while acoustic tones try to soothe said beasts; California comes up with a nicely-flowing bass line and Kotleba's synth flourishes punctuate Randy's strong vocals.

'Bionic Unit' (California, Fowley, Mooney, 2:52)

'Bionic Unit' is the second song on *Future Games* co-credited to Hollywood provocateur, producer, musician, and songwriter Kim Fowley, the Svengali manager of 1970s-era female rockers the Runaways and a notorious 'man about town'. I'm not sure what Fowley might have brought to the song, which sounds like a pseudo-techno version of Randy's normal (i.e. trademarked) future visions, with swirling synths, sci-fi lyrics reminiscent of Robert Heinlein, and more than a casual nod to the *Star Trek* TV series, of which California was obviously a fan.

'So Happy Now' (California, 0:19)

A brief interlude with movie dialogue, a distant Randy vocal riff, and a quick segue into the upcoming Dylan cover.

'All Along The Watchtower' (Bob Dylan, 4:27)

California returns to Dylan by way of Hendrix, taking his mentor's well-worn reading of 'All Along The Watchtower' and re-imagining the song with Cassidy's tribal drumbeats, tense electric guitars, hollow, distant vocals, and dropped-in movie/TV dialogue and other odd sounds found around the studio. It's miles away from either Bob or Jimi, but strangely alluring, and you can't argue that Randy found a way to provide the classic rock song with his own unique imprint. Probably too anarchic even for FM radio in 1976 (which by then was adopting stricter, more conservative playlists like its AM kissing cousin), California's performance here is nevertheless stunning and poetic in an entirely experimental manner.

'Would You Believe' (California, 3:13)

Opening with snippets of *Star Trek* dialogue, the cult TV show obviously had a profound effect on California, and there's no doubt that the show's multi-racial cast and hippie ethos of a peaceful universe seemed like an aspirational dream to the spiritual seeker in California. With distorted washes of humming guitar and wistful vocals, Randy delivers a strong and hopeful set of lyrics:

> Would you believe in people smiling starships on the ground,
> Would you believe all understanding coming from the sound,
> Would you believe in people turning away from the dreary past,
> And looking towards a future shining of a love that will last.

With a taut guitar riff and mournful voice, California dives into his own dream for the future, ending 'Would You Believe' with the plaintive lyrics 'would you believe a heart that's crying for your very soul, would you believe I care about you, more than you know'. It's a powerfully emotional performance filled with yearning, part of which is expressed with Randy's voice, part with his lyrics, and part with his guitar.

'Jack Bond Speaks' (California, Burt Shonberg, 1:17)
California's artist friend Burt Shonberg returns, with this lofty ode delivered with finely-crafted guitar and lofty lyrics, Shonberg's 'Jack Bond' alter ego barging in at the end with studio-altered vocals and a spacey message for the future generation.

'Star Trek Dreaming' (California, 2:16)
California crosses the streams here, blending his *Star Trek* fandom with the album-opening CB radio references, fighting through the fog of the opening intro noise to settle into a steady groove textured by flaming guitars and some odd synth effects, Randy again incorporating sample dialogue from the TV show into a musical format.

'Interlude XM' (California, 0:26)
Another short interlude with found sounds surrounded by slashes of music. Genius or madman? You decide...but by building 'songs' around sampled dialogue (i.e. transformative 'fair use' under U.S. copyright law), California earned a few extra (badly-needed) cents per album in publishing royalties.

'China Doll' (California, Cassidy, 2:00)
A short, albeit confusing song, 'China Doll' opens with a vaguely-Asian instrumental pattern, Randy singing of his 'China Doll' in the first verse ('she was only five foot tall, she walked in style, loved me for a while, now she's gone and I need her') before switching gears and talking about 'Chairman Mau' (Mao?) above the same ticky-tacky soundtrack. While you're still scratching your head, California walks us out with a profound 'time is ticking, the clock on the wall is ticking for us all...'

'Hawaiian Times' (California, 0:10)
Meh … a few more cents in California's publishing royalty account (see below…).

'Gorn Attack' (California, Timothy Blanton, 2:10)
California dives back into the *Star Trek* universe (the Gorn were a humanoid reptilian alien from the TV show) with this engaging fever dream of a song, a mixed bag of discordant piano and plucky surf-inspired guitar that leads into the acid-drenched lyrics: 'loosening your grip on pain living in a soundless dream, nothing is ever real, your body goes numb and dumb, and hollow is what you feel'. Amazingly, 'Gorn Attack' and both the preceding and following interludes blend into a single hallucinogenic dream on record.

'Interlude 2001' (California, 0:25)
Round and round we go, dropping coins into the bank for show (see above…).

'Detroit City' (California, Cassidy, 3:55)
A bluesy little shuffle with a heavy bass line, Cassidy's brushed cymbals and wiggy six-string courtesy of Mr. California, 'Detroit City' was evidently based on a true story. California's lyrics are fun and self-referential – 'well the people, they were happy, 'cause they knew they'd been somewhere, took a magic trip with Spirit, so their minds wouldn't even care' – and don't take themselves too seriously. Randy fumbles the ending, though, with a chaotic callback to 'Bionic Unit', backwards-tracked vocals, and a bunch of other noise leading out of the song.

'Freakout Frog' (California, Cassidy, 1:57)
You have to wonder if California didn't come up with much of *Future Games* after binge-watching Saturday morning teevee. It's like the boy downed too many bowls of chocolate-frosted sugar bombs cereal and, experiencing a rush of energy and enthusiasm, ran off to the studio. Here he samples Kermit the Frog from the *Sesame Street* TV show to lead into a wacky song about the heroic 'Freakout Frog' with helium-voiced lyrics accompanied by joyful synthesizers and weird, gauzy fretwork. You just can't hate a song with a chorus of 'ribbit, ribbit', though…

'The Romulan Experience' (California, 0:57)
California reads Star Trek dialogue in his own studio-altered voice, packing a lot of musical ideas into a tight one-minute window, drenching the vocals in reverb, galloping drumbeats, and spacey guitar buzz (and calling back to 'All Along The Watchtower').

'Monkey See, Monkey Do' (California, 1:39)
A soulful diversion from California's high-tech hijinks, 'Monkey See, Monkey Do' is a too-short R&B tune with soulful vocals, distaff backing harmonies,

stellar guitar trappings, and engaging percussive work. It seems too half-baked, however, and if the song's pop undercurrent had been fleshed out another minute or so with an extra verse and guitar solo, it might have been an AM radio winner.

'Mt. Olympus' (California, 0:25)
California's innovative studio-spun blend of radio DJ patter, advertising snippets, scraps of TV dialogue and other found sounds presages not only the inspired sampling of early hip-hop pioneers like Kurtis Blow, Grandmaster Flash, The Beastie Boys, et al. but would also influence new wave and avant-garde musicians years down the road. By this point on *Future Games*, however, the gimmick is merely irritating, comprising better than a third of the album's tracklist.

'The Journal Of Nomad' (California, Tom Hall, 2:30)
An intriguing instrumental that builds upon a sturdy, recurring rhythmic track with clamorous piano, livewire double-tracked guitars, and elements of musical themes pulled from throughout *Future Games*, 'The Journal Of Nomad' is the sort of edgy, admirable musical elegy that John Locke used to provide Spirit albums.

'Ending' (California, 3:50)
A fitting coda to the creative roller-coaster ride that is *Future Games*, California's 'Ending' calls back to several other songs from the album before spinning into a sort of talking blues song about the attack on Pearl Harbor that launched American involvement in World War II. The song offers some brilliant, poetic imagery – 'the emperor's heroes flying on high, while they drop their death wish on the shore, the sounds of panic, no mercy filled the air' – but Randy's closing lines, patriotically jingoistic, are artistically at odds with his hippie persona that nearly a decade of Spirit songs have showcased. The song fizzles out with the same Hawaiian native tune that opens the album, closing out a confusing, albeit entertaining, album.

The Adventures Of Kaptain Kopter & Commander Cassidy In Potato Land (1981)

Personnel:
Randy California: vocals, guitar, bass, miscellaneous devices
Ed Cassidy: drums, percussion
Additional personnel:
George Valuck, Mike Bunnell, Karl Nile, John Locke: keyboards
Jeff Jarvis: trumpet
Mike Thornburgh: horns
Chuck Snyder: saxophone
Joe Green: saxophone, strings
Mike Bunnell: string and horn arrangements
Producers: Randy California, Michael Lee, Robert Lee
Engineers: Robert Lee, Bob Burnham, Dennis Chobanian, Mike Stone, Gary Brandt
Label: US: Rhino Records, UK: Beggars Banquet
Release date: 1981
Current edition: UK: Retroworld Records, 2011 (CD)

Wow, where do I start? After his near-tragic equestrian accident and resultant head injury, Randy hung around Southern California, writing new songs and performing around L.A. It was during this period - while the Staehely Brothers were on the road with the pseudo Spirit - that California came up with his Kaptain Kopter alter ego and recorded his 1972 solo debut *Kapt. Kopter And The (Fabulous) Twirly Birds*, with some talented friends. The album underperformed commercially at the time, but has since become a cult classic among a certain sect of masochistic rock fans (like yours truly).

Evidently California's solo debut sold well enough for Epic to ask for another, so Randy went into the studio with stepdad Ed and a group of even-more-talented friends to pursue a loose-knit Orwellian concept about an oppressed country called Potato Land, which had been rattling around his damaged skull. Originally to be released in May 1973 as *Back Together Again*, Epic Record executives gave the album (subtitled 'The Adventures of Kapt. Kopter and Commander Cassidy') a cursory listen, and said no, subsequently hiding the master tapes deep in the bowels of the dungeons beneath its Madison Avenue offices.

This California/Cassidy recording became known as one of the great lost rock albums of the 1970s; a great white whale for the hardcore faithful. Cassette copies circulated freely among Spirit fans, most likely sourced from a BBC radio broadcast by DJ Bob Harris, who hosted California and Cassidy on his show and played a rough-hewn acetate copy of the unreleased album on air: much to the delight of home tapers across the UK.

Rhino Records released an abridged version of the album, with the title *The Adventures Of Kaptain Kopter & Commander Cassidy In Potato Land* on vinyl in 1981 under the Spirit name, with an underground comic-inspired cover and interior artwork by Craig Moore. As Randy had lost the original master tapes, he worked from an acetate copy and introduced overdubs and re-recordings, including songs not originally intended for the album, creating a rather disjointed feel to the Rhino Records version. To call the resulting album quirky would be an understatement, but Spirit archivist Mick Skidmore sums it up best in his liner notes to *The Original Potato Land*: calling out Epic Records for its refusal to release the LP: 'Given the kind of material that Frank Zappa was putting out at the time, it mystifies that Epic rejected the album and dropped the band from the label. I believe the album would have been a huge hit at the time, and who knows where that would have led?'

Though it was never meant to be a Spirit album *per se*, but rather a California and Cassidy record, it might've been a bit cheeky for Rhino to release it under the band name. But as the pair basically *were* Spirit for the better part of 20 years, maybe it wasn't that audacious. The original truncated single-disc version of *Potato Land,* released by Rhino Records and Beggars Banquet, was superseded by the expanded Acadia 2006 CD reissue titled *The Original Potato Land,* and later by Retroworld's 2011 two-disc set (see the compilation-albums chapter for more info). In keeping with Skidmore's chosen nomenclature, I'll refer to the album as *Potato Land* throughout this chapter; it's just as commonly referred to as *Potatoland*.

'We've Got A Lot To Learn' (California, Cassidy) (2:11)
Opening with a melodic guitar part, trumpets and the prerequisite 'doo doo doo' hook, this is a pop song at heart; sounding a little like George Harrison's 'My Sweet Lord.' There's a lot of Beatles flavor, and a groovy set of Randy's hippie-lovin' lyrics that land softly on your ears. Altogether it would've been a decent-enough single for 1972/1973 - a little lighter than legacy Spirit, but enchanting nonetheless.

'Potato Land Theme' (California, Cassidy) (5:02)
Randy had a mid-decade penchant for funk-infused rhythms, and, naturally, drummer extraordinaire Ed was more than up to the challenge. The problem with these flights of fancy was that once Cass laid down the groove, California often didn't know what to do with it. 'Potato Land Theme' is as ludicrous as entire concept, with nonsensical lyrics and odd voices. But Randy's twangy chicken-pickin' is spot-on, sounding like Ernie Isley of The Isley Brothers (and another Hendrix protégé), but with less ambition. Thankfully, the horns are funky but subtle, and don't override the foot-shufflin' rhythms.

'Open Up Your Heart' (California, Cassidy) (4:51)
An intricate multitracked guitar pattern leads into a droning vocal mixed high above the various instrumental textures. Though the breathless speak-sing gets a little tiring, the thick instrumentation nearly salvages what's an otherwise

Above: Spirit live on stage circa late 1967 or early 1968. (*Mick Skidmore/Randy C. Wolfe Trust*)

Below: Signed photo of the original Spirit line-up. (*Mick Skidmore/Randy C. Wolfe Trust*)

Left: Spirit's self-titled debut album with a cool composite photo of all four band members by Guy Webster. (*Sony Music*)

Right: Spirit's sophomore effort, *The Family That Plays Together*, featured the band's lone chart hit, 'I Got A Line On You'. Cover photo by Guy Webster. (*Sony Music*)

Left: *Clear*, the hastily constructed third Spirit album with cover photo by Guy Webster. (*Sony Music*)

Right: The trippy, psych-drenched cover artwork of the band's undisputed masterpiece, *Twelve Dreams Of Dr. Sardonicus*. (*Esoteric Recordings*)

Left: Is it 'very, very good' or is it 'lousy'? Cover art for the controversial *Feedback* album featuring the Staehely brothers. (*Sony Music*)

Right: The 'comeback' album, *Spirit of '76*, features front and rear cover artwork by LA artist Burt 'Jack Bond' Shonberg. (*Mercury Records*)

Left: A hodgepodge of stylistic experimentation and pop architecture, *Son Of Spirit* is a Randy California solo album in disguise. (*Mercury Records*)

Right: Marking a partial reunion of the original band (sans singer Jay Ferguson), *Farther Along* is a flawed, artistically weak album that nevertheless opened the door for the superior *Spirit Of '84*. (*Mercury Records*)

Left: Assembled from solo recordings and studio experimentation, *Future Games* is a maddening, meandering, but entertaining album that displays both California's creative excesses and his virtually limitless imagination. (*Mercury Records*)

Right: Resurrecting the 'lost' Spirit album, Rhino Records enlisted artist Craig Moore to provide an underground comix-styled cover for *The Adventures of Kaptain Kopter & Commander Cassidy In Potato Land.* (*Rhino Records*)

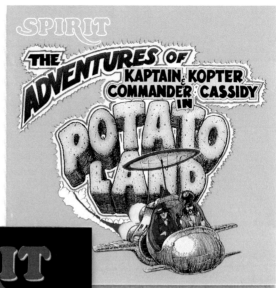

Left: A new coat of paint for an old album, Acadia Records' *The Original Potato Land* CD reissue. (*Acadia Records*)

Right: For their final reunion, Spirit reworked seven classic songs on *Spirit Of '84* (along with three new tunes), imbuing the old gems with a slick 1980s-era sheen and a fresh energy. (*Mercury Records*)

Left: Show poster for Spirit's headline spot at The Rainbow Theatre in London circa 1978. (*Esoteric Recordings*)

Left: Randy California and his guitar circa 1979. (*Mick Skidmore/Randy C. Wolfe Trust*)

Right: Spirit guitarist Randy California on the cover of the UK publication *The History of Rock*. (*author's collection*)

Below: Phonogram Records' promotional photo for the band's *Spirit Of '84* album. (*Phonogram Records*)

Left: Spirit's *The Thirteenth Dream* (released in North America as *Spirit Of '84*) was one of the first digital recordings of the CD age, shown here with the oddball cover art of the European version. (*Phonogram Records*)

Right: A transitional recording and the band's lone I.R.S. Records release, *Rapture In The Chamber* has its charms and is well worth another listen. (*I.R.S. Records*)

Left: Original lo-fi cover art for the independently-released *Tent Of Miracles* album, photo by Ed Cassidy taken in London, 1990. (*Line Records*)

Right: Equally cool cosmic cover art for the deluxe 2020 CD reissue of *Tent Of Miracles*. (*Esoteric Recordings*)

Left: The original wiggy *California Blues* cover art, digitally manipulated and incorporating photos by Ira Cohen and Steve Aguilar. (*W.E.R.C. C.R.E.W. Records*)

Right: Acadia's deluxe expanded two-disc CD reissue of *California Blues* features a fierce action shot of Randy California on stage. (*Acadia Records*)

Left: The independent and fearless mid-1980s Spirit line-up. (*Mick Skidmore/Randy C. Wolfe Trust*)

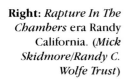

Right: *Rapture In The Chambers* era Randy California. (*Mick Skidmore/Randy C. Wolfe Trust*)

Left: The family that plays together – Spirit circa 1996 for the *California Blues* album. (*Mick Skidmore/Randy C. Wolfe Trust*)

Right: Randy California's auspicious debut LP, *Kapt. Kopter And The (Fabulous Twirly Birds)* with cover photo by Bud Lee. (*Sony Music*)

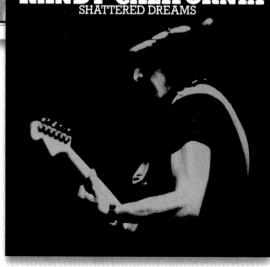

Left: This cover photo for *Euro-American*, Randy California's second solo effort, attempts to catch both sides of the singer, songwriter, and guitarist's personality. (*Line Records*)

Right: Cover artwork for the aptly-titled third and final Randy California solo album, *Shattered Dreams*. (*Line Records*)

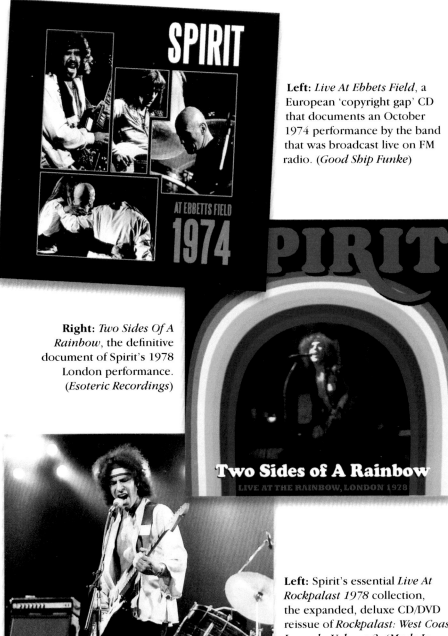

Left: *Live At Ebbets Field*, a European 'copyright gap' CD that documents an October 1974 performance by the band that was broadcast live on FM radio. (*Good Ship Funke*)

Right: *Two Sides Of A Rainbow*, the definitive document of Spirit's 1978 London performance. (*Esoteric Recordings*)

Left: Spirit's essential *Live At Rockpalast 1978* collection, the expanded, deluxe CD/DVD reissue of *Rockpalast: West Coast Legends, Volume 3*. (*Made In Germany Records*)

Right: Featuring rare recordings from Spirit's earliest performances, *Live At The Ash Grove 1967* was recorded by the band's friend Barry Hansen, better known as Dr. Demento. (*Flashback Records*)

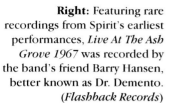

Left: The band's first live CD release, *Live At La Paloma*, with suitably psychedelic cover art incorporating photos by Andy Sopczyk. (*W.E.R.C. C.R.E.W. Records*)

Right: Reintroducing the band to American audiences, Spirit's *Time Circle 1968-1972* compilation album. (*Sony Music*)

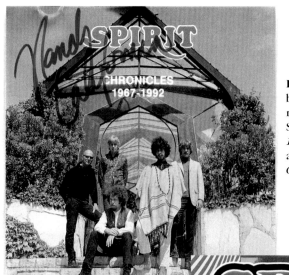

Left: Taking advantage of the buzz around *Time Circle*, Randy released his own collection of Spirit tunes, *Chronicles 1968-1992*. Autographed copy from author's collection. (*W.E.R.C. C.R.E.W. Records*)

Right: A color-splashed *Cosmic Smile*, the first posthumous Randy California/Spirit CD with a cool cover by noted concert poster artist Mark Arminski. (*Phoenix Gems*)

Left: Sundazed Records' loving 2000 tribute to early Spirit, the *Eventide* vinyl compilation. (*Sundazed Records*)

Right: Cover of the second of Sundazed's excellent Spirit compilations, *Now Or Anywhere*, released in 2000. (*Sundazed Records*)

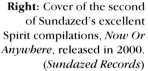

Left: *Blues From The Soul* is a posthumous two-disc 'odds 'n' sods' compilation pieced together by Mick Skidmore from various tapes and featuring a wonderful cover photo by Steve Aguilar. (*Acadia Records*)

Right: *Tales From The Westside* serves up two discs chock-full of 1990s-era Spirit performances with a cool action shot of Randy and Ed on the front cover. (*Floating World Records*)

Left: Cover model Ed Cassidy, music zine from author's collection. (*Worldly Remains*)

Right: *Model Shop*, Spirit's ill-fated soundtrack album for French filmmaker Jacques Demy's American movie debut. (*Sundazed Records*)

Left: Eye-catching picture sleeve for the 1984 single release of 'Mr. Skin' from the *Spirit Of '84* album. (*Phonogram Records*)

mundane song. For no reason whatsoever, a marching band comes tramping across at about three minutes in, adding to the confusion, before a giant wave splashes in and washes everything away.

'Morning Light' (California, Cassidy) (3:40)

In a similar pop/rock vein as 'We've Got A Lot To Learn, the lyric outlines a lovely boy/girl dynamic. But the studio-altered vocal doesn't fit, and the instrumentation is too busy, too chaotic and too scattershot to make this appear as more than a throwaway.

'Potato Land Prelude' (California, Cassidy) (2:13)

Amidst a swirl of turbo-charged synthesizers and shards of electric guitar, this eschews the pompous funk of 'Potato Land Theme' in favor of an electronic pastiche that would've sounded at home on a Utopia LP. Still, it's awe-inspiring in its own peculiar way, with a tsunami of random notes riding on oscillating waves until the explosive conclusion.

'Potato Land Introduction' (Mike Bunnell) (2:25)

This mostly spoken-word piece is an oddball construction, with found vocals, sounds and inspirations, weaving their way into something you might hear from The Firesign Theatre. The lyric theme is a sort of *1984*/*Brave New World*-styled satire that, surprisingly, didn't entirely originate from Randy's fevered brain.

'Turn To The Right' (California, Cassidy) (1:21)

Another Firesign-inspired track, with a spoken intro that quickly devolves into a sort of Oompa-Loompa acid trip. The ominous beginning veers into a sort-of rockabilly stomper with swaggering vocals, blasts of horn, flamethrower guitar and an overall bluesy vibe that grabs you by the ears and refuses to let go. Randy sums up the 1970s zeitgeist, singing, 'Turn to the left, then turn to the right/Well there ain't no love baby, nowhere in sight.'

'Donut House' (California, Cassidy) (5:46)

With an explosion, found vocals and blasts of laser fire and electronic squiggles, this morphs into soft-shoe vocals, light Cassidy brush work and crazy-quilt lyrics that will take the listener years to decipher. Randy's livewire fretwork takes the song into the stratosphere, and the lines 'Well the queen of hearts, she was catching on fire/While the grapefruit begged the 'tow away' sign' showcase California at his most maddeningly Dylanesque. Also, it seems that the man *really* liked his chocolate eclairs.

'Fish Fry Road' (California, Cassidy) (3:55)

I'm beginning to sense a culinary theme, and now we've landed in hot oil on 'Fish Fry Road', the song sporting a now-prerequisite conversational opening, crackling flames and a crying baby. After all, that mess moves out of the way, it blows up into a cool, hard-rocking track with rapid-fire vocals, raging horn play, stunning guitars and Cassidy's big beat all mixed into a grand slurry of instrumentation. What it's about is anybody's guess ('So don't give me your shoeshine or your two stepped mister/I don't need no polished shoes'), and near the end, it suddenly drops into a piano riff from *Twelve Dreams*.

'Information' (California, Cassidy) (4:11)
'Wow, that sure was a bizarre scene back there, man!,' says Randy, opening 'Information' above the return of the dreaded Oompa-Loompa rhythm. The guys see a giant potato shaped like a telephone, where you can get 'Potato Land information. Dialing a pre-destined number, our hero gets the lowdown on *Potato Land*. Man, there's not enough weed in the world to make sense of these lyrics. Maybe Potato Land is an analogy for the USA: 'For we only allow dullness in this place.'

'My Friend' (California, Cassidy) (3:47)
The album concludes with a wonderful, red-hot slab of power pop that dates back to Randy's days with The Red Roosters. With an underlying British-Invasion groove, he builds a truly-enchanting musical moment with jangling tambourines, molten guitar licks and a locomotive rhythm track, while he sings of lost love: 'Well, go looking for a guy that treats you better than I/And maybe then you'll look in my eyes, realize that I love you.' Then the song abruptly changes course into a bit of bloated hype about the next album and 'the revenge of the French fries.' At a mere 38 minutes plus, *Potato Land* seems long on half-baked ideas and short on substance - a situation that would be partially redeemed by the expanded *The Original Potato Land*, which provided greater insight into Randy's madness.

Spirit Of '84/The Thirteenth Dream (1984)

Personnel:
Randy California: vocals, guitar
Jay Ferguson: vocals, guitar
Mark Andes: bass, vocals
John Locke: keyboards
Ed Cassidy: drums, percussion
Additional personnel:
Matt Andes, Bob Welch: guitar, vocals
Curly Smith: drums, percussion, vocals
Keith Knudson: drums, percussion
Bruce Gary, Alan Gratzer: percussion, vocals
Joe Lala, Bobby La Kind: percussion
Jeff Baxter, Howard Lesse, Gary Myrick: guitar
Neal Doughty: keyboards
Jerry Jumonville: saxophone
Producer: David De Vore
Engineers: Alan Sides, Mark Ettel, Mark Richardson
Label: Mercury Records
Release date: June 1984
Current edition: UK: BGO Records, 2005 (CD)

Spirit's second (and final) *reunion* was a full-blown affair, with singer Jay Ferguson back in the fold for another shot at glory on what is essentially a *covers* album, with the band re-recording seven of its classic songs alongside three shiny new tunes. Before you turn the page, though, know that these are solid reworkings of the old gems, with a slick 1980s sheen and a fresh energy and enthusiasm that was lacking from the band's previous reunion effort *Farther Along*.

Recorded in December 1982 for an audiophile label and originally titled *The Thirteenth Dream*, this was one of the first digital recordings of the CD age, and the album's excellent fidelity stands head-and-shoulders above much of Spirit's early recordings. Phonogram signed the band for a four-record deal (which never worked out), and Mercury released the album on CD in West Germany in 1984. Mercury released it on vinyl in the US, and renamed it *Spirit Of '84* (though I like the title *The Thirteenth Dream* better), with less eye-catching cover art. A reworked version of 'Elijah' was recorded during these sessions, but was not included on the releases.

With a (presumably) decent budget to work with, the band recorded at A&M in Hollywood with producer Dave DeVore at the helm. (He'd previously engineered albums by artists like Nils Lofgren, Grateful Dead and Alice Cooper.) Though the sound is a little thin at times and largely ignores the band's typically-fat bottom end, DeVore did a decent enough job with what was then cutting-edge digital technology. A truckload of guest musicians were brought in, including superstars like Jeff 'Skunk' Baxter (Steely Dan) and Bob Welch (Fleetwood Mac), though I'm not sure why they needed them or what they actually contributed.

Mercury released 'Mr. Skin' b/w 'Fresh Garbage' as the album's first single, and I remember the label putting some promotional muscle behind the album at the time, even releasing 'I Got A Line On You' b/w 'Black Satin Nights' as a second single, to no avail. The album failed to chart, and the label forgot they'd ever signed the band. It's a shame, and I see it as a case of missed opportunity. How could they not release '1984' (described by writer Alan Robinson in the reissue liner notes as 'A fine piece of paranoiac pop') in 1984, at the tail-end President Ronald Reagan's first term? Robinson concluded his notes by saying, 'The new tracks aren't quite the ticket, and after a mini-tour of shows on the West Coast in August 1984, Ferguson, Andes and Locke all returned to other commitments, leaving Cassidy and California to pick up the Spirit baton.' Though I largely agree with the esteemed Mr. Robinson (publicist for Nick Lowe, Elvis Costello, Gary Moore and others) about the three new songs, I truly believe that 'Pick It Up' would've been a wise choice for the second single, maybe with 'All Over The World' as its B-side rather than going back to the well one more time with the otherwise-classic 'I Got A Line On You.'

Reassessment of the album has not been kind. In his review of Spirit's *Sunrise And Salvation* box set for *Ugly Things* magazine, Steve Krakow writes of *The Thirteenth Dream*: 'It's just pretty awful. Featuring limp and kinda bloated re-recordings of earlier hits, and studio musicians galore, the bonus live material from '85 is just as tepid.' Stalwart Spirit fan William Ruhlmann wrote in his AllMusic review: 'As it was, the album was dominated by the remakes, which, not surprisingly, were inferior to the original recordings, but which served to remind listeners how good those recordings had been ... It had the feel of a victory lap, but for a band that never quite won the prize in the first place.'

Jay Ferguson spoke of the band's mid-1980s reunion shows in *Worldly Things* zine in 2001: 'They were great. I think everybody came in with no expectations, there was no pressure, and everybody really had this bury-the-hatchet attitude ... there was a lot of mutual appreciation and a lot of love. So, these reunions were little mini love fests for us.'

'Black Satin Nights' (Ferguson) (3:12)
This new Spirit song opens with crescendos of crazed synths and Cassidy's bombing-run drum rhythms, the song spinning off into the sort of Aquanet-drenched, big-haired nerf-metal hard rock that the mid-decade spawned. Ferguson's vocal rides up-front with the band's harmonies in the rumble seat, while the lyrics are typically inane for the era. It sounds a lot like a late-period Ferguson solo effort, though Randy does do a scorching two-minute solo. It's not bad, not great, not really Spirit in spirit.

'Mr. Skin' (Ferguson) (3:39)

Re-recording one of their most popular songs (Ferguson's ode to Spirit godfather Ed Cassidy), the band couldn't stray too far off the path, and they didn't. Sure, there are a few new instrumental flourishes shoehorned in, and the vocals (lead and harmony) are nowhere near as dynamic and effective as on the original. The production seems a little trebly in spots, and Jerry Jumonville's sax solo is a bit wonky for my taste, but it's a decent-enough updating of the classic song.

'Mechanical World' (Andes, Ferguson) (5:50)

In contrast, this stern remake is aces, taking the song's innate alienation and machine-like strides to a whole other level. The slightly-altered arrangement pushes the vocal up front, the torch six-string supports the overall mood of despair, and the heavy-plodding percussion and fleshed-out instrumentation displays the band's experience and talent. If *this* version had been a single in 1984, it could've ruled the world.

'Pick It Up' (Ferguson) (3:00)

Another new song, this displays all the studio tricks of the early-1980s, without a syrupy lyric like that of 'Black Satin Nights' to hold it back. A hard rockin' romp, the band cuts loose with the instrumental thunder and lightning, California's guitar solo cuts nicely, Locke plays the 88s like he's banging away in a Mississippi juke joint, and the rapid-fire vocal matches the overall locomotion. It was a timely effort, and another lost opportunity for a hit single. (What *was* Mercury thinking at the time?)

'All Over The World' (California, David Crawford, Lisa Henke) (3:57)

The third and final new song is obviously by Randy, and not just because his lighter vocal and acoustic-guitar opening. It's a wonderful slab of too-late hippie ethos, but a lovely mid-tempo ballad with elegant fretwork and classically-cool piano, coupled with California's hopeful refrain, 'And all the kids in the '60s were yelling peace and freedom for all/It's starting all over again, it's happening all over the world.'

'1984' (California) (3:59)

Opening with the sound of whirling helicopter rotors, the first burst blows through the door like an angry S.W.A.T. team, before the familiar ominous bass line kicks in. Of all the versions of this controversial song, this is probably my favorite. It doesn't differ wildly from the original, but it is fleshed out, with more barbed wire and hidden corners; the band sleeker and just as dangerously hungry as they were a decade earlier. Another horrible corporate oversight was Mercury dropping the ball here by not releasing '1984' as a single at the time.

'Uncle Jack' (Ferguson) (2:59)

Again, the band's shared experience and prowess with their tools show up in spades on this re-recording of the psychedelic-era favorite. If anything, it sounds even more like late-period psych rock than the original, with bright vocal harmonies, better stereo separation effects, and an overall impulsive British-Invasion vibe. Writing for AllMusic, critic Matthew Greenwald calls the song 'A powerful psychedelic rocker ... another great example of Spirit's ability to build a song around a riff.'

'Nature's Way' (California) (2:44)

It would be hard to re-imagine this ecology ode any better than the classically-inspired instrumental version on *Farther Along*, but this take is a fine effort nonetheless. Even more dreamy and out there than the original, Cassidy's steady percussion sets the tone while the musicians embroider with their instrumental magic. Softer, more-lofty and yet more urgent than the original, the message was just as important in 1984 as it was ten years previous.

'Fresh Garbage' (Ferguson) (3:05)

How can you remake a classic of minimalist angst like 'Fresh Garbage' in the 1980s? Bolder and brasher, that's how. The familiar mesmerizing riff remains, but it's been jazzed-up and spazzed-out with riotous instrumentation, razor-blade guitar licks, hairy synth riffs and a new group chorus that descends into chaos. Overall, it's a complete overhaul of the song for a new and demanding decade - one that showcase's the band's immense collective imagination and willingness to explore new avenues of rock 'n' roll a decade and a half after their founding.

'I Got A Line On You' (California) (7:34)

Not quite a complete makeover, but varied just enough to catch your ear, this rollicking revisiting of the band's only hit, dials the already intense arrangement up a notch. The guitar solos sting a little deeper, Cassidy's percussion is harder-hitting, and the entire band's commitment to the ideal resulting in a too-cool-for-school instrumental break that channels exotic percussion into a hard-rock frame. It won't replace the original take in the ears of longtime Spirit fans, but it might've been enough to attract some newcomers to the California cult of personality.

Rapture In The Chambers (1989)

Personnel:
Randy California: vocals, guitar
John Locke: keyboards, effects
Ed Cassidy: drums, percussion
Additional Personnel:
Mark Andes: bass ('Hard Love', 'Enchanted Forest')
Janet Wolfe: backing vocals
Curley Smith: drums ('Hard Love')
Producer: Randy California
Engineers: Scott Campbell, Mike Nile
Label: I.R.S. Records
Release date: 1989

Rapture In The Chambers was, in many ways, a transitional recording, leading
to what many consider to be Spirit's late-period classic *Tent Of Miracles*.
Randy came to the attention of Miles Copeland and I.R.S. Records after
performing at the label's Night of the Guitar events alongside fellow guitar
slingers like Leslie West, Alvin Lee, Steve Howe and Robby Krieger (See the
'Live Album' section for more info). The concerts were distilled down to a
two-album set for release in late 1989. Randy is represented by 'Hey Joe' and
a performance of his song 'Groove Thing' with Hunter.

Copeland was seemingly looking for the harder version of Spirit for his
label, not dissimilar to Randy's sound on his solo LP *Restless*. And in a year
when rockers like Metallica, Living Colour and Aerosmith shared the top of
the charts with middle-of-the-road and soft rock artists like Madonna, Phil
Collins and Roxette, a new Spirit album seemed like a safe bet. Recorded at
Mike Nile's Malibu studio Nileland, California, Cassidy, Locke (with Randy's
sister Janet Wolfe on backing vocals), the album is maddeningly erratic,
jumping from melodic pop to hard rock and acoustic ballads in the blink of
an eye, never staying with one style too long.

Sadly, I.R.S. never put much promotion behind *Rapture*, and the results
were predictable - the album didn't reach the charts. It was a one-off deal that
didn't help boost the band, and the record soon went out of print, where
it has languished for over 30 years. Though it stands solidly in the middle
of the Spirit catalog in terms of creativity and satisfaction, the album has its
moments and is deserving of another listen. AllMusic critic William Ruhlmann
certainly thought so, writing in his reassessment:

> The album lacks the musical diversity that was typical of records by the
> original band. California constructs good rock tunes that showcase his
> exceptional lead guitar-playing, and he writes lyrics that refer to common
> romantic concerns, promote environmental ideas or seek spiritual uplift.
> *Rapture In the Chambers* is a more-consistent effort than the Spirit albums

of the mid-'70s that California helmed. But fans of the original lineup will hear only echoes of the band's early sound.

'Hard Love' (Andes, California) (3:18)
Co-writer Mark Andes was the bassist for Heart, and Randy coaxed him to play on this song, with former Jo Jo Gunne bandmate Curly Smith on drums. Andes crafted a radio-ready track, rocking just enough to satisfy the punters but with a melodic pop hook punctuated by Randy's subtle guitar licks. The romantic lyric is all Randy's, describing the difficulties plaguing many relationships: 'It's so hard when time rearranges the feelings in our hearts' and 'So many times I've tried to leave girl/But my heart only knows why I stay'. Randy's soft crooned is supported with synth flourishes and electronic orchestration. The charts were open to diversity in 1989, and 'Hard Love' could've fit on FM alongside any Skid Row or Guns N' Roses power ballad. But without any significant radio airplay, it was a tough slog.

'Love Tonight' (California) (2:45)
This album was another display of California's ability to move with musical trends, even though he always seemed to be a man out of time. 'Love Tonight' is a perfect example - Randy crafting a big guitar sound for an otherwise rote hard rocker (not unlike the aforementioned Skid Row and their ilk) with inane lyrics (ditto). Sadly, this sound had peaked commercially a couple of years earlier, and was about to get curb-stomped into oblivion by raw-boned Pacific Northwest longhairs with loud guitars and plaid shirts.

'Thinking Of' (California) (4:10)
Randy returns to his comfort zone here with an acoustic ballad with imaginative six-string wrangling and oblique - albeit poetic - lyrics. 'Alone like a pillar in a forgotten garden filled with nature's abundant gifts' is a cool opening line; California crossing his never-ending spiritual quest with eco-friendly imagery for a folk 1960s-ish song that nevertheless sounds contemporary. Part of me wishes we could've heard the full original Spirit record the song.

'Rapture In The Chambers' (California) (3:15)
With a complete change of direction, the title track is a synth-dominated electro-rocker with thoughtful lyrics and lofty vocals more aptly-suited to a song like 'Thinking Of.' Randy's critique of the mindless pursuit of wealth ('More than often they speak with a forked tongue/More than often they look but never see')would fit better as either a mid-tempo acoustic ballad or an unbridled hard rocker instead of this industrial-tinged pop, but at least California plays a couple of decent solos amidst the buzz and hum.

'Mojo Man' (California) (2:29)
A fusion of the good old Spirit and the forward-facing trying-to-get-a-record-deal band, 'Mojo Man' is a lot of fun. Mixing a hip-hop lyric flow and a tongue-

in-cheek romantic tale taking inspiration from a dozen old blues songs ('Too much talking and too much balking/Sitting in the corner with your red dress on'), it recalls a lot of late 1970s-era Mitch Ryder - a golden age when the greatest of rock's blue-eyed soul singers opened for Bob Seger at a nine-night homestand in Detroit.

'Contact' (Locke, California) (2:42)
John Locke's fingerprints are all over this stinker, which blends 1980s synth-pop like OMD or New Order, with electric funk and soul (I'm thinking Prince); Randy's multitracked guitars layered on like too much icing on a too-small cake. It's a trifle of a song, suiting his spoken/sung vocal style, but he's too talented and eclectic to resort to this pale Gary Numan imitation.

'The Prisoner' (California) (4:16)
A lengthy story song with brilliant lyric imagery ('He's counting the ways, each day goes by/Year after year he knows, but he doesn't know why/He lives for his dreams'), accompanied by shards of blistering guitar, backed by Locke's obsessive synth-pop backing track. California's erstwhile 'Prisoner' could just as easily be himself, or any of us, feeling trapped by life's cruel games while searching for a better way. 'Dreams come and come/He rides the stars to a distant sun' could've been Randy's theme song.

'One Track Mind' (California) (3:22)
Randy lets his freak flag fly with a guitar-heavy mid-tempo rocker that flashes lyrical brilliance at times. His six-string patterns and textures override Locke's wandering synthesizers, and Cassidy's drums are finally noticeable - they've been largely AWOL for much of the album; they're there but atypically overshadowed. Overall, it's just an average hard rocker, not necessarily contemporary or faddish. But oh, those guitars.

'Enchanted Forest' (California) (3:28)
This - the album's creative apex - is Randy California at his inspired best. Musically it's eclectic, from acoustic ballad to electric rocker, with shades of baroque pop and soft-psych, and had some of the most well-written and literary words from Randy to that point. 'He swears he's gonna try before he dies, to take those heart-sung chances' is another great opening line, and it ties in perfectly with the closing 'Back in the world of reality/Concrete canyons are all he sees/Childhood memories, so far back when/He wonders what his life could have been.' In between these verses, Randy explores a lot of emotional territory, his words and vocals supported by a gorgeous, subtle backing track reminiscent of early-Spirit.

'Human Sexuality' (California) (2:56)
Lyrically sparse (There are only 18 words) and musically eccentric, 'Human Sexuality' finds its inspiration in British electropop, with its synthesized

rhythms, rudimentary drums and stultifying overall arrangement. It's not particularly trendy and not especially entertaining, though there are a couple of nice guitar lines hidden within.

'She-Ra Princess Of Power' (California, Locke, Cassidy) (4:35)

California channels his fanboy fascination to pen an ode to the cartoon heroine with all the gravitas the title suggests. It's an interesting idea, but lacks in execution - heavy on backing vocals and Locke's intermittent piano notes, with Randy's guitar chiming in from time to time. Otherwise, it's no more than interesting filler, with a slight lyric and an even slighter performance.

'End Suite' (California, Cassidy) (1:28)

The obligatory instrumental (every Spirit album has at least one), 'End Suite' is a dynamic, multi-hued musical exercise, with some found vocals floating by and various changes that stretch at least a minute beyond the CD's listed track time of 1:28.

Tent Of Miracles (1990)

Personnel:
Randy California: vocals, guitar
Mike Nile: bass, vocals
Ed Cassidy: drums, vocals
Producer: Randy California
Engineer: Kevin Gray
Label: US: Dolphin Records, Germany: Line Records
Release date: 1990
Esoteric Recordings reissue produced by Mick Skidmore
Current edition: UK: Esoteric Recordings, 2020 (CD)

The roots of this album come from circa 1989 at a club in Trancas Beach, Malibu, California, where a band, including former Spirit keyboardist Scott Monahan and bassist Mike Nile, played. Randy California frequently dropped by to jam, attracting A-list musicians like Eddie Van Halen to come and watch, according to Nile. California recorded several of his solo songs with Nile's backing band, and later incorporated Nile into Spirit. Nile was no stranger to Spirit, having co-engineered *Rapture In The Chambers*, and contributed to *Potato Land* under his real name Mike Bunnell. *Tent Of Miracles* was recorded at Nile's Nileland studio - shorn of the synthesizers and production sheen of *Rapture*, it was a more-organic stripped-down meat-and-potatoes album.

In 1990, singles by folks like Madonna, Sinead O'Connor and MC Hammer dominated the charts, while hard rock was represented by artists like Guns N' Roses, The Black Crowes and Living Colour. Grunge was beginning to bubble up and make waves in Seattle with bands like Temple Of The Dog and Mother Love Bone, but it would be almost a year before Nirvana broke the bank with their ten-times-platinum-selling *Nevermind* album - jump-starting a label feeding-frenzy that vaulted the Pacific Northwest to superstar status for most of the decade.

It was into this environment that Spirit released *Tent Of Miracles* on their own independent label Dolphin Records; their friends at Line Records in Germany issuing the CD in Europe. Both *Tent Of Miracles* and the equally-impressive *California Blues* (1996) were to be caught in the marketplace meat grinder, overshadowed by pop, boy bands and plaid-clad rockers like Pearl Jam and Soundgarden, who were selling in multi-platinum numbers. But Spirit - sitting on two of their best albums since the 1970s - couldn't get a major label to buy them a cup of coffee and a pastry.

Band archivist and producer Mick Skidmore relates in the *Tent Of Miracles* liner notes that Randy sent a tape of three new songs to Arista Records head Clive Davis, in an attempt to get a fresh deal. Davis replied: 'I listened to the material from the new Spirit album, and I'm sorry to say that I didn't think the songs were very meaningful.' Randy challenged Davis to send him 'meaningful' albums by Arista artists like Barry Manilow and Milli Vanilli. Spirit's major-label days were clearly behind them, along with the financial support and promotional possibilities that such a relationship implied.

With *Tent Of Miracles* all but ignored upon its release, critical reappraisal has been kind to the fan favorite. Critic Joe Viglione writes in AllMusic:

> *Tent Of Miracles* is one of the best Spirit albums by the trio version of the act ... more serious and refined than the Mercury Records releases in the mid-'70s. Decades on the road touring, along with having those highly experimental albums behind them, make this a very musical and mature chapter ... *Tent Of Miracles* holds many secrets, and is that extension of *Twelve Dreams Of Dr. Sardonicus* that California was seeking for so many years.

The album's expanded Esoteric Recordings 2020 reissue adds a whopping nine bonus tracks, and includes a second disc of a 16-song live performance from 13 March 1990 at The Melkweg, Amsterdam in support of the *Rapture* album. The set incudes older Spirit songs like 'Fresh Garbage', 'Nature's Way' and 'Mr. Skin,' while also road-testing new ones like 'Tent Of Miracles' and 'Zandu'. It also has dynamite performances of material from *Rapture,* including the title track and 'Love Tonight.'

In compiling the tracklist for the expanded *Tent Of Miracles,* Skidmore utilized alternate versions of eight of the album's 12 songs. He wrote in the CD liner notes: 'I delved into the archives, where I found many DATs and several reels that contained various mixes and takes of a lot of the tracks. So in assembling this reissue, I took the liberty of going through them and ended up choosing a number of alternative or unedited versions, which I thought gave the album a more cohesive feel.'

Of the album's original independent release, Skidmore says, 'It may have been presented with something of a low-budget feel - mostly due to the lo-tech artwork - but there was nothing shabby about the music.' Indeed, California feels invigorated here, sharing the songwriting burden with the creatively-fresh Nile, instead concentrating on six-string flights of fancy. *Tent Of Miracles* stands as one of the band's best late-period releases, and is an enduring fan favorite.

'Borderline' (Cassidy) (2:10)

A brief, mad-dashing instrumental, opens the album. It's credited to Mr. Skin, though it's clearly a group effort. No matter, as it's a pulse-quickening romp with Cassidy's tribal 'I Want Candy'-style rhythms galloping throughout, as Randy's guitar swoops and dives with reckless abandon; shards of glassine notes giving way to a classy, jazz-like finish. It's a proper roller-coaster ride.

'Zandu' (California) (4:29)

Dating back to the band's late-1970s era, this late-period fan favorite is nevertheless short on melody, and serves more as a showcase for California's six-string virtuosity. The spiritual lyrics are punctuated by guitar squawks and marching rhythms; the syncopation and whiplash time signatures making for an interesting if unspectacular performance.

'Love From Here' (California) (4:17)

With a rhythmic opening reminiscent of Grand Funk Railroad's cover of the Soul Brothers Six song 'Some Kind Of Wonderful,' and with elements borrowed from Randy's 'One By One' and 'The Blues', he quickly embroiders with mystical guitar and ethereal lyrics, establishing the song as a bluesy take on love, romance and the search for peace. The multitracked guitars often seem to be pulling in different directions. But listen a few times and you'll hear they're all telling the same story from varying perspectives. It's a superb display of Randy's composition skills.

'Ship Of Fools' (Nile) (4:33)

Bassist Mike Nile contributed four songs to *Tent Of Miracles,* and to his credit, he tried to write authentic Spirit songs. Nile said in the CD liner notes, 'I deliberately tried to write a song that fitted Spirit's sound,' and on three of his four songs, he did just that. 'Ship Of Fools' is a neat little low-slung blues-breaker with an opening barbed-wire guitar lick and Nile's solid-steel bass lines, which take more than a little inspiration from Willie Dixon's 'Superstition': a favorite of transatlantic blues rock bands. Nile's vocals here are decent enough, but there's something missing amidst the bluster.

'Burning Love' (California) (3:09)

A mid-tempo rocker with brightly-shining guitars, an infectious recurring rhythm, partially-buried vocals and a strong bass presence. 'Burning Love' is the epitome of the 1970s power trio creation, updated for the grungy 1990s. Nobody is going to mistake Spirit for Soundgarden, or even Alice In Chains at this late date in the band's history, but this track is a dense, riff-heavy rock song that could've held its own in the ring with those bands.

'Tent Of Miracles' (Nile) (5:57)

This is Nile's second song on the album, and he nails the Spirit sound with a funky bass lick, overlaid with California's gold-standard guitar lines, a syncopated rhythm and accompanying vocal cadence. As a satirical take on modern society and religion, it ain't half bad, and Randy asserts himself, spitting out the lyrics like they're holy scripture, while the boys keep the foot-shuffling Bo Diddley beat rolling in the background.

'Logical Answers' (California) (3:27)

This opens kind of bluesy with an extended intro full of rumbling bass, fluid guitar patterns, echoing chords and a malevolent swamp-blues vibe, before changing direction completely into a sort of country-fried protest song. A gentle acoustic strum serves as a bridge between the two musical camps, and

Randy's singsong lyric calls for logical answers to issues such as homelessness, hunger, poverty and crime. Who knew that California was in favor of a 10% flat tax (probably the only thing he has in common with publisher/politician Steve Forbes). The music is a little faux twang, and the melody a bit simple, but the lyric is heartfelt and honest in its naivete. Listen for the rare vocal cameo from drummer and Spirit lifer Ed Cassidy.

'Old Black Magic' (Nile) (3:21)
Nile's anodyne vocals dominate on an otherwise early entry to the 1990s funk revival. With a hip-swaying rhythm, dancing bass line, blasts of horn, a braggadocio lyric and a strutting demeanor, it's really hard to believe that this is a Spirit song. Apart from the obligatory guitar solos, Randy is buried in the mix, creating the album's only miscue.

'Neglected Emotion' (California) (2:04)
This is a mid-tempo ballad recalling Spirit's 1980s songwriting direction. California's lovelorn lyric is poetic, the vocal is delivered breathlessly, and the modicum of guitar is tasteful, *nay*, elegant in stature.

'Imaginary Mask' (California, Cassidy, Nile) (2:25)
The album's only group-written song here is a fine example of a late-period Spirit studio jam. Randy soft-peddles the vocal, and threads his filigree guitar work throughout, while Nile's hefty bass notes hold down the bottom line and Cassidy adds some jazz flourishes.

'Stuttgart Says Good-bye' (California, Cassidy) (7:07)
Above a staggered drum rhythm and a walking bass line, California delivers a rambling stream-of-consciousness lyric with a few romantic overtures thrown in for good measure, while the other two guys hum along in harmony behind him. It's not dissimilar to American-Indian activist John Trudell's poetic rants set to music (Check out Trudell's 1986 album *aka Graffiti Man* featuring phenomenal guitarist Jesse Ed Davis), but has amped-up absurdity combined with a strangely alluring cacophony and a shimmering rainbow finish. Though derived from a studio jam, Nile was not given a songwriting credit.

'Deep In This Land' (Nile) (3:55)
The original album went 12 songs deep, with this one being Mike Nile's finest contribution to the album, barely beating the impressive 'Tent Of Miracles.' A raging rocker with laser-focused guitars soaring above a rock-solid rhythm, Nile delivers an acceptably-audacious hard rock vocal, while Randy's guitar screeches, roars and soars behind like a caged beast suddenly set free. Murky enough for the burgeoning grunge era - but rocking hard enough to reach the Guns N' Roses nerf-metal audience - 'Deep In This Land' could've been a solid single in 1990, straddling as it did, the sharp edge between hard rock and soft metal.

Bonus Tracks:
'Covered Wagon' (California) (2:14)
Skidmore dug up a number of bonus tracks for the album's 2020 expanded reissue, and 'Covered Wagon' is definitely one of the most curious. With a country sound, spry guitar pickin' and lyrics inspired by TV westerns, the song is an unusual addition to the Spirit milieu but not an entirely unwelcome one: growing on you with subsequent listens.

'California Band' (California) (2:58)
This is a fun, self-referential, semi-biographical life-on-the-road jaunt with ringing guitars and an unrelenting rhythmic background. If it sounds familiar, it is - it's a faster version of Spirit's 'California Man,' with different lyrics.

'Zandu' (California) (4:32)
A slower version than that on the original album, this has a droning vocal and sparse percussion. I can see why Randy used the fleshed-out version on the album, as this one was taken out of the oven far too soon.

'Kokomo' (Mississippi Fred McDowell) (3:02)
This reverent cover of the Mississippi Hill Country blues legend's signature tune would've been preferable to Nile's 'Old Black Magic' on the album. Randy's guitar turn here is stunning - his nimble fingers matching the fast lyrical delivery, rollicking bass line and Cassidy's imaginative percussion choices.

'All I Need Is Time' (California) (5:02)
This charming acoustic demo with lo-fi sound would've been another fine album addition. Sporting an endearing lyric accompanied by an appealing guitar strum, if you added drums and bass, you'd have a gleaming example of California's poetic sensitivity. Skidmore found this one on an unmarked cassette tape, and correctly chose to rescue the almost-lost gem.

'I Can't Dance No More' (Live) (Nile) (2:57)
The expanded reissue closes disc one with four live tracks from a March 1994 gig in Park City, Utah. This one is a Chicago blues swinger with scorching fretwork and Mike Nile's fine, lusty, growling vocal turn.

'Dark Eyed Woman' (Live) (California, Ferguson) (3:46)
Reaching back to 1969's *Clear* for this deep cut, the three-piece 1990s Spirit still managed to bring fire to the sultry song. Randy's slow-burning vocal is accompanied by his dark-hued guitar tone and Cassidy's explosive percussion.

'Woke Up This Morning' (Live) (California) (5:08)
In the CD liner notes, Skidmore describes this as 'impromptu,' and indeed, it sounds like a half-written, partial idea, with a bluesy lyric that would

embarrass the worst bar-band hack, and perfunctory guitar work falling short of California's talents and his status as the Stevie Ray Vaughan of psychedelic rock.

'Borderline' (Live) (Cassidy) (3:08)

In a neat bit of symmetry, disc one of the expanded reissue closes with this live performance of the album's opening song. Though it's missing some of the romping dynamics, the live setting displays more spontaneity and energy.

California Blues (1996)

Personnel:
Randy California: vocals, guitar
Rachel Andes: vocals
Matt Andes: slide guitar, vocals
Steve Loria: bass, vocals
Ed Cassidy: drums, percussion, vocals
Additional Personnel:
John Locke, Scott Monahan: keyboards
Arthur Barrow: bass ('Pawn Shop Blues')
Denise Gula: strings ('Pawn Shop Blues')
Todd Smallwood: guitar ('One World')
Robbie Krieger: guitar ('Sugar Mama')
Spencer Davis: guitar; vocals ('Gimme Some Lovin'')
Bruce Gary: drums ('Gimme Some Lovin'')
Bob Nichols: drums ('The River')
Michael Lewis: horn arrangements
Producer: Randy California
Engineer: Steve Loria
Label: W.E.R.C. Crew Records
Release date: 3 December 1996

Spirit's 14th and final studio album - due to Randy California's tragic death a month after the album's release - was also the band's first studio effort in six years. California returned to his roots with a collection of blues-inspired originals and a brace of well-chosen covers, by his mentor Jimi Hendrix, and legendary bluesmen Howlin' Wolf, Robert Johnson and the duo of Sonny Terry and Brownie McGhee, who Randy knew personally from his time hanging around his uncle's club. It's a solid record with fine performances, and guest appearances from talents like The Doors' Robbie Krieger and British Invasion legend Spencer Davis.

California Blues was recorded with a core band of California, drummer Cassidy, and bassist Steve 'Liberty' Loria, who also engineered and mixed the album with Randy producing. Several members of the Spirit family also contributed, including keyboardists John Locke and Scott Monahan, who appear on four and three songs, respectively. Matt Andes adds his scorching slide guitar to several tracks, and his 15-year-old daughter Rachel sings on a number of songs. Overall, *California Blues* was a fine follow-up to *Tent Of Miracles*, and proof that Randy still had a lot of great music in him just waiting to be expressed.

As was usual with Spirit albums at this time (and for the previous two decades, actually), there were few (if any) reviews. The reviews found floating around the internet these days are largely retrospective, such as critic and obvious Spirit fan William Ruhlmann, who wrote about the album for AllMusic:

'Rachel Andes' vocals are a good addition on the new songs - particularly the acoustic ballad 'Call On Me,' which is a duet between her and California. *California Blues* includes some excellent Randy California guitar-playing, and suggests new directions for Spirit that - unfortunately - the band would never be able to pursue, as well as featuring entertaining guest performances and historical curios.'

Oddly enough, one of the most insightful online reviews of *California Blues* comes from an anonymous, self-described 'prog folk researcher' by the name of Clem of Nazareth: 'The music here isn't as important as the fact that California finally seemed to have found peace after many years of personal struggle and lack of recognition for his inspiring songwriting skills, and for his incredible oneness with the guitar,' pointing out that Randy's 'idealistic lyrics seem out of place today - indeed they kind of seemed out of place when he wrote many of them ... but he was never a slave to fashion, preferring instead to make a path in his own way and let the rest of us get on board, or not.'

In 2009 there was an expanded two-disc reissue titled *California Blues Redux*, through Audio Fidelity in the US and Acadia Records in the UK and Europe. But sadly, both have been out of print for over a decade, and are now harder to find than the original W.E.R.C. Crew CD release. The *Redux* version is worth buying - the set expanding the first disc with an additional seven bonus tracks, and adding a second disc of live performances from roughly the same period, and featuring several songs from the studio work. *California Blues Redux* was curated and produced by the ever-reliable Mick Skidmore.

'California Blues' (California) (3:48)
Randy's guitar screams like a wolverine caught in a steel trap, Ed Cassidy's cowbell rides in on hooves of thunder, and multitracked guitars spin out of control. This mesmerizing effect is only partially broken by Rachel Andes' backing vocals, which don't mesh well with California's already downplayed voice. It's a fun song nonetheless, with several styles of screeching fretwork, judicious use of horns (i.e. not too many, just enough...), and an overall up-tempo rockin' arrangement that'll get yer foot stompin'!

'Look Over Yonder' (Jimi Hendrix) (2:35)
There's a deep dive into Jimi's songbook here with this rowdy, creative cover: an often-overlooked gem from the legendary guitarist's *Rainbow Bridge* movie soundtrack. Randy imbues the song with new energy, coaxing from his guitar a different sonic signature than usual; his cool-as-a-cucumber vocal, inspired, and running in place with his machine-gun guitar licks. There are some superfluous backing vocals, but they don't matter, 'cause Randy simply slays the song!

'The River' (California) (4:22)
Things cool down with this low 'n' slow spiritual with spry acoustic guitar, church-choir vocal harmonies and an overall reverent-seeker vibe that's just

one step removed from Randy's hippie roots. It's a little bit of blues, a little bit of Gospel and a whole lotta soul, with some golden guitar playing to help wash down the message.

'Call On Me' (California) (2:58)

Rachel Andes' voice works better here as a lead instrument in a lovely duet, her gossamer vocal offering a distinctive counterpoint to California's more plaintive tone. He gives a gorgeous acoustic guitar performance here to match the song's romantic tilt, and if Spirit had been on even an indie label with juice, this track could've been a hit single on Adult Contemporary radio.

'Crossroads' (Robert Johnson) (5:46)

Mississippi Delta blues legend Robert Johnson recorded 'Cross Road Blues' in San Antonio, Texas in November 1936 for the Vocalion label, and the song went on to become an influential blues standard. Elmore James reshaped the song as 'Standing At The Crossroads' for his own purposes in 1960 - a version likely heard by young British guitarist Eric Clapton, whose version of the song (as 'Crossroads') with his band Cream was to popularize Johnson's blues with rock audiences. Rockers The Doors, Ry Cooder, The Allman Brothers Band, Lynyrd Skynyrd, Johnny Winter and many others have recorded the song over the ensuing years.

It's a short jump from Cooder to California, and Spirit's version here skews closer to Cream's electrified take than to Johnson's original. However, some important instrumental flourishes separate Randy *et al.* from the rabble of cover monkeys and chart seekers - from Steve Lora's heavyweight bass lines and Cassidy's rumbling tom-toms to Randy's bluesy vocals and straight-razor guitar solos that rival those on Clapton's version for intensity. Throw in a false ending and rebound, Loria's bass virtuosity and a sludge-like overall tempo nearing stoner metal turf, and you have an entertaining reading of an often-abused blues gem.

'Song For Clyde' (California) (5:40)

The blues vibe continues with the rambling 'Song For Clyde', which features Grateful Dead-style vocals, a rolling rhythmic groove and a lighthearted arrangement that surrounds California's voice with a cushion of instrumentation. He plays around in the studio here, adding slight vocal effects and panning his solo from one side to another to interesting effect.

'Pawn Shop Blues' (Sonny Terry, Brownie McGhee) (2:48)

California draws on those many nights as a teen spent in the audience at The Ash Grove, studying antique bluesmen and bugging them for guitar tips and lessons after the show. This stellar cover of folk-blues duo Terry and McGhee's classic, shows that the backstage education paid off - Randy capturing the original song's strident cadence, adding a loping rhythm, a strong spoken/sung

vocal and scraps of electric guitar. All that's missing is somebody like Sugar
Blue adding blazing harmonica (strings are substituted instead) - then you'd
have a nearly perfect blues-rock fusion.

'Sugar Mama' (Chester Burnett) (3:18)

With his head definitely in a blues space for *California Blues*, Randy covers
this Howlin' Wolf' song by way of the Grateful Dead, with a languid 1960s-style
aura, laid-back percussion, and subdued-yet-stylish lead guitar courtesy of guest
Robby Krieger of The Doors: who nails the solo just the way Jerry would've
played it.

'Red House' (Hendrix) (6:12)

Jimi's 'Red House' is one of his most popular songs among the hardcore
faithful, so it's no surprise that Randy performed it from time to time. This live
version (circa 1993 from The La Paloma Theater in Encinitas, CA) takes the
best of Hendrix's original and stretches it out to six minutes of bluesy rock-
guitar jam and a slinky groove sure to please an audience. Though Randy's
voice lacks the inherent soul of Jimi's pipes, he acquits himself nicely with an
emotional performance perfectly matching the lyric to his incendiary fretwork,
while Cassidy shuffles along and Monahan's piano plays mournfully from the
depths of the arrangement.

'Gimme Some Lovin'' (Steve Winwood, Muff Winwood, Spencer Davis) (3:36)

Collaborating with British-Invasion hitmakers The Spencer Davis Group on this
remake of their monster hit, California and Davis don't so much as reimagine
the classic rock gem, as strip it down for parts and sell them at the flea market.
With an ominous looming bass line, an off-kilter rhythm track from drummer
Bruce Gary, electronically-altered vocals, and Davis' wiry guitar solos, it's an
entirely different creature to the Steve Winwood-sung version that hit number
2 in the UK and 7 in the US in 1966.

Bruce Gary is an interesting cat in his own right. Best-known perhaps for his
tenure with power pop outfit The Knack circa 1979/1980, Gary was in fact, an
in-demand session player who toured and recorded with talents like bluesmen
Albert Collins, Albert King, New Orleans music legend Dr. John, Jack Bruce of
Cream, singer-songwriter John Hiatt, and Robby Krieger of The Doors. Gary
was also a Grammy-nominated producer who worked extensively with the Jimi
Hendrix estate, assisting in the compilation of several posthumous albums, and
playing on earlier Spirit LPs like *The Thirteenth Dream*, and on Randy's solo
albums.

'We Believe' (California) (3:40)

Built on Steve Loria's walking bass line, with hints of guitar buzzing around the
edges, Randy and Rachel create an intriguing jazz undercurrent for what is an

otherwise half-baked idea. Neither vocalist has their voice mixed high, leaving the heavy lifting to Loria and Cassidy's jaunty rhythms. The performance gets better as it rolls along, with stronger vocals, but I can see a straight duet version as a stronger play.

'One World' (California, 3:44)
A snazzy white-hot slab of West Coast jump-blues with a semi-spiritual lyric, 'One World' benefits from Michael Lewis' horn arrangement, squalls of guitar notes, vocal harmonies, John Locke's joyful keyboards, and an infectious liver-quivering rhythm track that delivers a foot-stompin' good time.

Bonus Tracks:
'Like A Dog' (California) (1:42)
Is it really a bonus track if your album was only released on compact disc and not on vinyl - the former format allowing for more minutes of music than the latter, so there's not anything actually added? It's a conundrum for the philosophically minded perhaps, but all of the album's bonus tracks are crammed onto the end of 'One World' so that while they're all assigned their own running times, there's no separate IDs: just a few blank spots. Thus, 'One World' effectively runs for over 20 minutes. But it doesn't matter, as 'Like A Dog' is a scrappy, acoustic Piedmont-styled blues with a lyric using the imagery of a dog drowning in the ocean as a metaphor for trying to keep your head above water in real life. This is a stunningly prescient and disturbing lyric, given Randy's ultimate fate just a few short weeks after the album's release.

'Poem For John Lennon' (California) (6:25)
This gentle, meandering, instrumental with poem recitation has plenty of musical twists and turns. It's a loving pastiche performed in honor of an artist who had a major effect on Randy California, who wrote the words shortly after the former Beatle's tragic 1980 death. California's pop/jazz guitar-playing is the highlight of an overall lovely ode to a rock-'n'-roll legend.

'Shoes Back On' (California) (3:15)
The last three bonus tracks are low-fidelity live performances from 1967 at L.A.'s The Magic Mushroom club, recorded by band friend Barry Hansen. The sound quality is hit-or-miss but not horrible, and not surprising considering the age and condition of the tapes. 'Shoes Back On' is an unremarkable slice of history - the sound of a band still finding its signature - and it's nothing to write home about.

'Tell Everyone' (California) (3:22)
Slightly better is this limping funk with Ferguson's muted vocal, jangling tambourine and sparse accompaniment that showcases the germ of a possible great song.

'Soundtrack For A Moth' (California) (2:37)

This is a discordant, messy, first-steps-towards-greatness instrumental jam, heavy on Locke's piano, with a kind of jazzy cacophonous blues sound that the band would later hone to a razor's edge. After a moment of silence, the album closes with roughly 30-seconds of familiar acoustic guitar patterns, serving as a fitting coda to Randy California's stewardship of the Spirit name.

More Bonus Tracks:
'Fixin' To Die' (Leadbelly, California) (2:26)

California Blues Redux offers a number of additional ultra-groovy bonus tracks, starting with this vital solo acoustic take on this song by country-blues legend Leadbelly, which here is imbued with a finely-weathered vocal and energetic guitar. California captures the Mississippi Delta here in both spirit and intent.

'Indian Girl Blues' (California, Andes) (5:51)

Co-writer Matt Andes adds slinky slide guitar in contrast with Randy's acoustic. It's a bit over the top with its humorous lyric and California's playful performance. I can see why it didn't make the original album, but it's a lot of fun nonetheless.

'Oriental Gun' (California) (2:54)

Producer Skidmore searched through California's seemingly bottomless stash of digital audio tapes, and came up with several tracks recorded during the same period as *California Blues* that would've otherwise been lost. This is a DAT-sourced performance, Randy and his guitar running rampant, with a stream-of-consciousness lyric that name-checks John Kennedy, Richard Nixon and the CIA in a struggle for the soul of America. It's performed in a sort of strident 1960s folk style, with energetic acoustic guitar and a rapid-fire vocal delivery.

'Soup Jam' (California, Andes) (3:42)

The product of California and Andes' jamming while sitting around Andes' kitchen, Skidmore edited it down from a much longer performance. Less than four minutes of blinding instrumental heat from two grizzled veterans of the rock 'n' roll wars getting their blues groove on while sitting around the kitchen table, just isn't enough, though. It's worth digging up a copy of *California Blues Redux* just for this performance.

'David' (California) (1:52)

This showcase for Randy's elegant six-string skills (if you've gotten this far in the book and aren't convinced of his talent), is a delicate instrumental with a few exotic guitar patterns thrown in - the sort of thing that could've gotten him a contract with Windham Hill Records if he'd ever chosen to go the New-Age guru route.

'Kind And Gentle Life' (California) (2:54)

A lovely provocative performance with a bluesy vibe, great vocals and dynamic slide-guitar playing. Matt Andes was quoted in the *Redux* liner notes, saying, 'That's not me playing, it's Randy, and he is using a real-unusual tuning. I wish it had been me, because it's such a beautiful legacy to Randy. Randy had mellowed out into this lovely soul before he died. I just consider myself lucky to have been part of that.' Bonus points for the false ending and brief coda, which evokes nearly 30 years of Spirit in a mere few seconds.

The live bonus disc included with *California Blues Redux* is another justification for finding a copy of the CD. Skidmore pieces together various great performances from 1993, 1995 and 1996 for the eight songs here. The 11-minute instrumental intro to the 18-minute 'Love From Here' is a song in itself, and well worth the price of admission. Various blues covers - like 'Pawn Shop Blues,' Leadbelly's 'Stewball' and Hendrix's 'Red House' are juiced-up in a live environment, and California originals like 'One World' and 'We Believe' also benefit from the space and energy of performing live.

Model Shop (2005)

Personnel:
Randy California, Jay Ferguson: vocals, guitar
Mark Andes: bass, vocals
John Locke: keyboards
Ed Cassidy: drums, percussion
Producer: Lou Adler
Mastering: Bob Irwin
Release date: 2005
Current edition: US: Sundazed Records, 2005 (CD/LP)

'In many ways, this soundtrack to the Jacques Demy film *Model Shop* is the Spirit album that never was,' writes Mick Skidmore in this album's liner notes. French writer/director Demy's first English-language film *Model Shop* was released in 1969, and though it weaved narratives recalling his earlier continental films like *Lola* and *The Umbrellas of Cherbourg*, the low-budget drama *bombed* in the US, with little or no support from Columbia Pictures (then the parent company of Spirit's label Epic Records). Interestingly, Demy allegedly wanted a young American actor by the name of Harrison Ford to star in the film, but unconvinced by Ford's acting ability, Columbia coaxed the director into using Gary Lockwood (from *2001: A Space Odyssey*).

Spirit makes an appearance in *Model Shop*, which - in spite of its meager box office returns - has since been reassessed as one of Demy's most critically-underrated and neglected films. American director Quentin Tarantino has cited *Model Shop* as an inspiration for his hit 2019 movie *Once Upon A Time In Hollywood*.

Spirit recorded the largely-instrumental *Model Shop* soundtrack in 1968, in between sessions for *The Family That Plays Together* and *Clear*. No soundtrack album was released at the time, as Mark Andes refers to in the CD liner notes: 'The film was *so* bad, that I think in the end that Lou (Adler, the producer) and the band's manager decided not to bring too much attention to it. Everybody had expectations that what we were getting involved in would be a high-quality thing.'

Songs from the recording sessions have dribbled out over the years, appearing as bonus tracks on CD reissues of early Spirit albums, and on the *Time Circle* compilation. However, the discovery of the original mono tapes opened the door for Spirit fan Bob Irwin to release the album on his Sundazed Records label (on CD *and* vinyl!). Previously released recordings from *Model Shop* were typically alternate takes or new stereo mixes. The first Sundazed soundtrack offers seven previously-unreleased alternate versions of songs, three with different mixes, all in glorious mono. Skidmore wrote: 'The album is presented as close to what had originally been intended as the score to the film.' Most of the music here was improvised, and was jazz-oriented overall, and some of the sounds they created for *Model Shop* would later be incorporated into songs for *Clear*.

'The Moving Van' (Ferguson, Locke, California, Andes, Cassidy) (1:56)
Light cymbals, underlying piano and muted instrumentation, including vibes, help create a cool ambiance for this instrumental.

'Mellow Fellow' (Cassidy, Locke) (2:50)
A little more upbeat, this instrumental has a couple of passages recalling music from Frank Zappa's satirical film *200 Motels*. As the track digs into a rhythmic groove dominated by Locke's electric piano, California's fuzzy fretwork soars above the fray.

'Now Or Anywhere' (Ferguson, Locke, California, Andes, Cassidy) (4:39)
Plodding metal instrumentation and distant vocals create an otherworldly vibe that falls just a few (stumbled) steps away from Black Sabbath. It's an interesting musical direction, California's heavyweight guitar licks and Andes storm-cloud bass notes setting the stage for what's possibly Spirit's most malevolent song. What little melody there is, was taken from 'Dream Within A Dream' from the *The Family That Plays Together* sessions.

'Fog' (Ferguson, Locke, California, Andes, Cassidy) (2:24)
Another provocative instrumental, heavy on atmospheric haze, and reminiscent of *Caravanserai*-era Santana with its vaguely Middle Eastern tones and hypnotizing fretwork.

'Green Gorilla' (Ferguson, Locke, California, Andes, Cassidy) (2:13)
Possibly the closest song on the soundtrack to *Clear*-era Spirit, 'Green Gorilla' is a mid-tempo, mostly-instrumental rock-'n'-roll track with just a trace of oblique backing vocal. Evincing a fierce, funky groove and showcasing California's jazz licks and Andes' Jaco Pastorius-inspired bass-playing, it's not radio-ready but sure is fun.

'Model Shop I' (Ferguson, Locke, California, Andes, Cassidy) (2:01)
Opening with Randy's throwback guitar licks - which sound like a mid-1960s amalgam of blues and jazz with a Wes Montgomery flair - Andes' hearty bass line rises out of the mix, accompanied by Locke's nuanced and barely-there keyboards. It's minimalist in a European jazz kind of way.

'Model Shop II (Clear)' (Ferguson, Locke, California, Andes, Cassidy) (4:08)
A gentle, gorgeous, gossamer instrumental with stunning guitar playing, swells of orchestration, and a few unexpected percussive elements. This track wears its classical influences on its sleeve, but makes way for Randy's muted, albeit magnificent six-string contributions.

'The Rehearsal Theme' (Ferguson, Locke, California, Andes, Cassidy) (1:11)

Too short to clear the runway, maybe this is a truncated version of a longer effort. Cassidy's fine, evenhanded percussion accompanies jagged guitar licks and discordant piano that sucks you in and walks away before paying off.

'Song For Lola' (Ferguson, Locke, California, Andes, Cassidy) (5:47)

Andes gets the spotlight here, taking his bass to new heights with a rumbling, grumbling, speaker-shaking performance only partially illuminated by Locke's twinkling star-like vibes hidden deep in the mix. Andes' four strings speak loudly on this intro. The band later appropriated part of 'Song For Lola' for the *Clear* track 'Ice'.

'Eventide' (Locke) (3:56)

Another jazz-like instrumental, dominated by Locke's piano stylings and propped up by Cassidy's lounge-lizard percussion, which is heavy on the brushwork.

'Coral' (Locke) (4:22)

Previously released in a different version as a bonus track on the *Clear* CD reissue, this take of 'Coral' is less orchestrated and relies more heavily on Locke's percussion and Cassidy's rolling drum rhythms. But they keep the underlying harmony, and I can almost hear this coming out of a cinema's speakers as the film plays. However, the drum solo three minutes in is pure 1960s Ginger Baker-style, and is totally incongruous with the opening and closing portions.

'Aren't You Glad' (Ferguson) (5:25)

The soundtrack closes with this as a bonus track and is totally at odds with the rest of the (largely) instrumental LP. It's a stripped-down demo of the fleshed-out performance found on *The Family That Plays Together*, and is preferable in many ways to the final version. Shorn of Marty Paich's string arrangement, the song is tougher, raw-boned, and rocks harder in all the best ways, with stellar guitar playing and larger-than-life rhythms. A shocking end to an otherwise entertaining but unspectacular soundtrack.

Randy California Solo Albums
Kapt. Kopter and the (Fabulous) Twirly Birds (1972)

After the luke-warm commercial response to *Twelve Dreams Of Dr. Sardonicus*, Spirit split apart, with Cassidy and Locke famously recruiting the Staehely brothers and hitting the road to meet booking obligations, while also taking advantage of Epic Records' reissuing of Spirit's first two albums as a double set.

Meanwhile, California took time off from touring, to write songs and jam with around L.A, eventually record this album - his solo debut - with talents like former Jimi Hendrix Experience bassist Noel Redding (under the pseudonym Clit McTorius), drummer Leslie Sampson (aka Henry Manchovitz) from Redding's band Road, drummer Tim McGovern (later of The Motels) and bassist Charlie Bundy (who went on to play with Americana greats like Nanci Griffith and Guy Clark). The original eight-song vinyl was heavy on cover songs, with only three California originals, and the album evinced a more-fierce hard rock sound than Spirit ever had.

The ghost of Jimi Hendrix cast a long shadow over the album's creation, which wasn't quite two years removed his tragic 1970 death. More than a mentor to the young Randy Wolfe, Jimi also wrote the musical blueprint that Randy subsequently adapted to his own music for decades. As such, you can clearly hear Randy (just 21 years old when he recorded *Kapt. Kopter*) channeling Hendrix's innovative style throughout the album. Produced by California with help from engineer Roger Dollarhide, the guitarist could've benefited from an outside pair of ears to tone down his wilder inclinations.

Probably the least coherent Randy California's albums, *Kapt. Kopter* is, nevertheless, one of his most enduring and entertaining works. Despite its flaws, the performances are full of energy and promise for better things to come. In his 2001 *Worldly Remains* interview, Cassidy spoke of the album's making: 'Just go for broke was the concept. Just play like maniacs. Make some sense out of it. It was kind of like organized chaos.'

California formed an official Kapt. Kopter band to tour the album, enlisting Cassidy and bassist Larry 'Fuzzy' Knight for several Southern California club performances. However, this trio toured Europe under the name Spirit, as promoters sought to capitalize on the band's reputation rather than cater to the artist's solo ambitions. As gigs were easier to get as Spirit rather than Kapt. Kopter, the threesome soldiered on well into the 1980s.

Critical opinion of the album was definitely a mixed bag at the time if writers took notice of it at all. Legendary critic Robert Christgau *was* a fan, however, waxing effusive in his 1981 book *Christgau's Record Guide: Rock Albums of the Seventies*, writing, 'Almost universally dismissed as a lysergic self-indulgence, the departed Spirit's tunefully-distorted guitar (and vocal) showcase will grow on you if you give it half a chance; any Joe Walsh fan who lets it get by, never really liked the '60s to begin with. For sheer dense weirdness, it beats King Fripp, and if I had any passion for such things, I'm sure I'd love it.'

But in *The New Rolling Stone Record Guide*, critic Billy Altman stated, 'Even the reunions of Spirit - California's original group - were less outrageous than this.'

The album certainly had enough magic to become a cult favorite over the ensuing decades. For instance, 'Downer' shows Randy at his most Jimi-esque; the song an ever-spiralling-upward hard rocker built on his experimental guitar scape, effects-laden vocals, a recurring riff that sounds like madness put to music, and drummer Leslie Sampson pounding away with a hearty tribal rhythm. All of this is set against a dense, flamboyantly-psychedelic backdrop that includes former Jimi Hendrix Experience bassist Noel Redding and the wonders of a multitrack studio. Think of Hendrix circa *Electric Ladyland*, and you'll have some idea of where Randy was trying to go with what Jimi started.

In contrast, 'Devil' is more-reflective, performed slower, and heavier on the atmospherics, with only a few psychedelic trappings, but not completely shorn of electronic effects. With backing harmonies from bassist Charlie Bundy and drummer Tim McGovern, California gradually turns up the temperature with ever-more creative guitar solos swirling around. One of a pair of Beatles covers gracing the album, 'Day Tripper' is stripped, going full-bore psychedelic overkill in both performance and the effects-laden production. As the mind-warping sounds bounce around, the mix is loaded with screeching guitars, rapid-fire drums and soaring guitar solos.

The somewhat reverent reading of Paul Simon's solo hit 'Mother And Child Reunion' - seemingly the most unlikely cover to be found here - is strangely familiar yet worlds apart, due to a psych-drenched coat of paint. Fans and critics alike consider the final song 'Rainbow' to be one of California's best - a fine showcase for his creative guitar-playing, with engaging lyrics and a riff that grabs your ears and won't let go. With drums by stepdad Cassidy, California layers nice bass guitar alongside his lofty yet semi-hidden vocal, resulting in a semi-melodic psych-heavy song that's concise, rockin' and complex.

Unfortunately, in what's now a familiar story, Epic Records did little or nothing to promote *Kapt. Kopter*. After its September 1972 release, the label released a cover of Rufus Thomas' 'Walkin' The Dog' as a promotional single - the non-album track failing to gain any traction with radio, and Epic washed its hands of the entire project. Still, continued interest in the album has resulted in numerous CD and vinyl reissues; Spirit fans remaining fascinated with California's initial studio experiments.

Euro-American (1982)

Fronting a band that was essentially *Spirit lite*, California recruited his old bandmates Mark Andes and John Locke to play alongside keyboardist George Valuck and drummer Curley Smith at L.A.'s Magic Wand Studios for this long-awaited solo follow-up. Jay Ferguson dropped by to lend some backing vocals, Matt Andes and Tom Hall added slide guitar to a song each, and 'Fuzzy' Knight and Ed Cassidy playeded bass and drums on 'This Is The End' and 'Mon Ami.' Finding no buyers in the US, Beggars Banquet released *Euro-American* in the

UK, and Line Records in Germany. But all previous CD reissues have been rendered moot by the album's inclusion in *The Euro-American Years 1979-1983* box set.

From the first gorgeous notes, you can hear it's very different from *Kapt. Kopter* and *Potato Land*. 'Toy Guns' is a brilliant anti-gun/anti-violence ballad with fascinating guitar interplay, softer vocal harmonies and swooping orchestration that envelops the multitracked vocals. It's an inspiring socially-conscious performance that makes its point, and the line 'Millions killed and no one takes responsibility' is just as devastatingly relevant today as it was then. The mid-tempo ballad 'This Is The End' is a poppy flyweight, saved from new wave pretensions by California's spry fretwork. If they'd made a video for it, I can see MTV's early-1980s star-making power helping propel it to the charts' upper regions.

With swirling guitar licks, interesting time changes, Randy's distant vocals and Andes' complementary bass line, 'Rude Reaction' updates Spirit's trademark *Twelve Dreams* sonic blueprint for a new decade. It's a hearty rocker with pointed lyrics:

I can't call you my brother if you don't act like a friend
After all of your millions, you were all alone like a rolling stone
Tell me what did you do for me during all these years I spent in poverty

I'm not sure who Randy is writing about here (I suspect it may have been Lou Adler, whom California and Cassidy both had a longstanding beef with), but the venomous lyric is accompanied by a hard-rockin' track with exemplary cutting-edge guitar-playing.

The muscular rocker 'Calling You' is slightly more brainy than its predecessor - with bluesy guitars, a more complex backing track (incorporating Zeppelin-esque touches) with a syncopated rhythm, and a machine-gun vocal verging on rapping, delivering bawdy, romantic lyrics. It's the perfect lead-in to a rowdy cover of The Troggs' classic-rock diamond 'Wild Thing' - reimagined, but including the familiar recurring riff and melody. The rest of the arrangement is stripped down and rebuilt from the foundation, with drummer Curley Smith's solid but unspectacular timekeeping and California's dancing six-string.

Euro-American veers over the double yellow line into oncoming traffic with 'Easy Love', which can be best described as new-wave-meets-nerf-metal'. The aggressive singing, lusty lyric and incendiary guitar solos sound like the coming L.A. hair-metal bands like Poison or Motley Crüe, while the electronic flourishes read more like Human League. It's an odd inclusion here, sitting at odds with the other material - even the politically-charged semi-funk 'Fearless Leader' with its superfluous orchestration. Much better are 'Skull And Crossbones' - an unbridled rocker that makes a case for Randy's guitar-god status - and the fantastic, punkish, energetic 'Breakout', that's less a guitar showcase than a heat explosion.

With the exception of the tawdry 'Easy Love' and, perhaps, 'Fearless Leader,' *Euro-American* was an impressive solo effort from California, who, as co-producer, incorporated his guest musicians' talents into recording an ambitious, creative and timely collection of largely original material. Though his left-leaning socially-conscious personality shines through in places, absent are the hippie aphorisms and studio production trickery that rendered albums like *Potato Land* and *Future Games* semi-coherent and absolutely without commercial potential.

Interestingly, *Euro-American* earned California a headline spot at England's 1982 Glastonbury Festival, from which a lot of video exists on YouTube, including a cover of Dylan's 'Like A Rolling Stone.' The performance gained some notoriety at the time, as - famously - the power generator went down due to operator negligence (someone allegedly fell asleep stoned and didn't refill the fuel) - an unfortunate circumstance that drummer Preston Heyman took advantage of with a 20-minute drum solo sans amplification: the audience playing along by banging beer cans together and chanting until the electricity was restored.

Restless (1985)

Searching for a way to finally throw off the Spirit albatross that was seemingly the fate of his career, California recorded his third solo album - in numerous venues, including Preferred Sound and Yamaha Studios in Los Angeles, Phonogram Studios, Wessex Studios, Berwick Street Studios and Utopia Studios in London. In many ways, *Restless* is California's glam metal album, skewed musically towards the mid-1980s trends and heavily influenced by the then past-its-expiration-date New Wave of British Heavy Metal (NWOBHM), with a big guitar sound and overall instrumental histrionics.

Drummer Preston Heyman got Randy a deal with Phonogram to release the album in Europe on their legendary prog rock imprint Vertigo. But after performing a few unspectacular dates in the UK, Randy returned to the US, and toured under the Spirit name for the rest of his career.

Recording in so many locations, he availed himself of a number of talented musicians, including former bandmates Mark Andes and John Locke on the title track. California's band at the time also included bassist Neil Murray, drummer and old friend Curley Smith and keyboardist Adrian Lee.

Although album-opener 'Run To Your Lover' was to appear on *Shattered Dreams* in a different arrangement, this version offers more unhinged guitar solos, set against stereotypical mid-decade hard rock. Title track 'Restless Nights' is a potential movie-soundtrack anthem searching for a star to cling to, with buzzing synths, group vocals and laser-focused guitars shining brightly above an over-the-top instrumental backdrop.

This version of 'Second Child' would've definitely fit in with offerings by NWOBHM bands like Raven or Saxon, with its titanium-strength guitar solos, martial rhythms and fantasy-laden lyrics. 'Shane' is a big, brash, razor-sharp rocker, with drummer Ed Cassidy leading the charge with explosive percussion embroidered by Randy's flamethrower guitar riffs and a heavier-than-uranium bass line. The vocal verges on heavy-metal thunder: leather-lunged and rough-hewn like Judas Priest's Rob Halford or Iron Maiden's Bruce Dickinson.

'One Man's Heaven' is another intricate metal song, opening with chiming guitars and six-string lines showcasing Randy's guitar prowess. The performance fizzles out with his earthy vocal whisper unsuited for such a molten guitar onslaught. (His vocal style on 'Shane' would've worked magic here.) But there's no denying the heavy riff or the apt lyric.

The mesmerizing instrumental 'Murphy's Law' gives way to the featherweight mid-tempo ballad 'Camelot'. Though it features some intriguing guitar playing, it's nevertheless a bit more whimsical than the surrounding songs.

The wimpy gloss of 'Camelot' is quickly forgotten when the needle glides into 'Battlemarch Of The Overlords' - a heavy-hitting, Viking-esque instrumental with taut high-flying guitars and powerful tribal rhythms: Curley pounding the skins like Cassidy in his prime. The over-the-top 'Childhood's End' stomps and stammers like an amalgam of Iron Maiden and Black Sabbath with a dash of Zeppelin tossed in for balance. The song plods steadily along on Randy's hearty riff, with his vocal running the razor in counterpoint; both aspects surrounded by lush, dreamy instrumentation, soon punctuated by electrifying guitar solos.

There was an audience for this kind of smart hard rock/heavy metal in 1985, but neither Randy nor Vertigo could get a foothold with those listeners. Truthfully, by this time, Vertigo was long past its commercial glory days of groundbreaking early-1970s rockers like Uriah Heep, Thin Lizzy and Black Sabbath. The label essentially served as a home for those artists that Polygram had no idea what to do with, or those that already enjoyed a modicum of commercial success in the US (like Dio, Kiss and Rush), and the UK releases were a profitable afterthought of sorts. Vertigo had little or no promotional muscle, and while there were a handful of *Restless* songs that could've passed muster for US FM radio, few stateside Spirit fans had any idea the album even existed.

After being long out of print, Acadia Records reissued *Restless* on CD in 2003. A solid creative effort, the album is easily in the same league as *Euro-American*, with a handful of above-average songs and stunning fretwork worthy of acclaimed contemporary axe manglers like Eddie Van Halen, Steve Vai, or Yngwie Malmsteen. But it seemed like Randy's solo career could never take flight, no matter how many musical pathways he explored (and left his indelible mark on).

Shattered Dreams (1986)

Shattered Dreams was California's final self-described solo album. Subsequent efforts would fall under the Spirit' banner: i.e. Randy and Ed and whoever would play with them. It's a collection of odds and ends that primarily featured the guitarist's stage band of drummer Preston Hayman and bassist John 'Buggsy' Pearce. The album-opening live version of 'Hey Joe' is from a Spirit show at the Stadtpark Open Air Festival in May 1981, with a band of Cassidy, keyboardist George Valuck and bassist Steve Loria. The title track features Cassidy, bassist Larry Knight and keyboardist John Locke. Most of the album was recorded at Music Works and Pathway Studios in London; the title track at the familiar Magic Wand Studio in Los Angeles.

'Hey Joe' was a staple of California/Spirit live shows throughout the 1980s, and the guitarist always found new ways to dress up the old warhorse he learned at Jimi's knee all those years ago. This live take plays it straighter than most, although the extended intro is quite mesmerizing. The title track evinces a slight funk influence, with Knight's bass hopping and bopping in counterpoint to California's stellar guitar tone. Locke's piano chimes in around the edges, keyboards joust with the bass, and the inspired vocal makes the most of the lyric. It's an intriguing song, with a lot of instrumental flavors and changes, and California's closing solo, takes flight.

Dylan's 'All Along The Watchtower' (via Hendrix) is the album's only other cover: another well-worn soldier on Randy's regular setlist. He spruces it up a bit here with spacey laser guitars, spoken/sung vocals in various registers, and an almost martial rhythm track. It's not my favorite of Randy's versions of the song, but it certainly is interesting.

'Don't Bother Me' is a bit of a mess, with metallic guitars, rudimentary percussion and dense production that sinks the entire thing into a pool of molasses sonically. Randy's commentary on society and poverty is insightful, and his solos here are razor-sharp, but it's a case where less production would've created a better track.

'Downer' - re-recorded from Randy's first solo album - revs the engine and races down the track, fueled by jagged guitar licks, sledgehammer bass strikes and runaway percussion, providing the listener with a hard knock on the head. Whereas the *Restless* take of 'Second Child' was more molten metal, this reading fools you with a slight acoustic intro that's subsequently stomped to death by riff-happy, Sabbath-styled doom-'n'-gloom instrumentation. The vocal is a bit forced, sounding at times like a growly Alice Cooper. The drum rhythms are explosive, the lyric semi-autobiographical (closer to Lou Reed than anything Randy wrote for Spirit), and the guitars stun like a shot of pure rocket fuel.

'Killer Weed' is the outlier: a mostly failed experiment that never launches. But it still rocks hearty, with heavy rhythms and rumbling switchblade guitars. But Randy affects his shock-rock vocals and horror-film lyrics with a healthy dose of *Welcome To My Nightmare*-era Alice Cooper. Oddly, 'Toy Guns' from *Euro-American* is retitled 'Hand Guns' here, but it's essentially the same melodic pop song with a message, and a cool 'Little Wing'-style acoustic riff. An otherwise rote mid-tempo rocker with romantic overtures, 'Run To Your Lover' nevertheless offers big-beat drums, sparse guitar pyrotechnics, lofty backing vocals, and was period-perfect for the mid-1980s; California's songwriting chops expanding and adapting to the decade's new sound. If the *Restless* version was a Van Halen-esque middleweight with a dash of new-wave synth, this version is a titanium-clad heavyweight.

Shattered Dreams is a harder-rocking effort overall, with a higher good-vs.-bad song ratio than either *Euro-American* or *Restless* - which isn't surprising, as it's comprised of material from the same era and sessions. Sadly, the album fell on deaf ears in 1986. Germany's Line Records reissued it on CD in 1997 as part of a two-disc set with *Euro-American, Shattered Dreams* was never released in the US.

KFPK Radio LA (2015)

'Take your clothes off and turn the volume up, ladies and gentlemen. This could be good!' That's the DJ's intro to this live radio broadcast of a September 1972 performance by Kapt. Kopter & the (Fabulous) Twirly Birds on Los Angeles radio station KFPK-FM. Cyprus label Keyhole Records released this nine-song CD in Europe. Keyhole specializes in unofficial vintage live radio broadcasts, and has issued similar recordings by several West Coast US artists, including Frank Zappa, Captain Beefheart and Moby Grape. The sound quality is decent enough for a 1972 recording, possibly sourced from a station soundboard tape, with some echo and a fair amount of hollowness but little distortion. It's the band's performance that stands out, though.

The Twirly Birds then included Knight and Cassidy, and the trio was performing locally in support of the recently-released *Kapt. Kopter* album. As such, the setlist is loaded with songs from the LP, including the funky James Brown cover 'I Don't Want Nobody', California's beguiling original 'Devil', the raucous 'Downer', and the Rufus Thomas cover 'Walkin' The Dog'. A number of the tracks have never seen release anywhere else - like the rowdy cover of the Jr. Walker & the All Stars hit 'Shotgun' (with spicy guitar licks mimicking Walker's saxophone), the spacey (mostly) instrumental acid trip 'Melting Into The Furniture' (a simply *fantastic* song title!), and the equally trippy cover of The Rolling Stones' 'Happy' which has a lengthy instrumental intro featuring raging percussion, dancing bass lines and California's least judicious use of electronic effects to that point.

The performance is challenging, entertaining, and either five years behind the psychedelic era, or so far ahead of its time that we haven't caught up yet. The CD booklet reproduces an interesting - albeit uncredited - April 1973 *New Music Express* Randy interview where he talks about Spirit and the Twirly Birds LP. More than half of *KFPK Radio LA* is unreleased material, providing another piece of the Spirit jigsaw puzzle.

The Euro-American Years 1979-1983 (2021)

Credited to 'Randy California & Spirit' (The two were pretty much inseparable at this point), this six-CD box set from the good folks at the UK archival label Esoteric Recordings, provides an exhaustive array of California's solo efforts and Spirit-branded performances from 1979 and the early-1980s. Compiled by the ever-reliable Mr. Skidmore, the first disc features the *Euro-American* album in its entirety. Rare outtakes and California's initial demos were only included on the French issue. The second disc offers various Randy solo and cover songs

- some of which subsequently appeared on *Shattered Dreams* and *Relentless*. But the album ends with the previously-unreleased 'Overloaded Ships Sink' - an odd, new-wave-ish song with unbridled electronics that would've sounded more like Ultravox than Spirit were it not for California's wistful vocals and gleaming fretwork.

Disc three has scraps of various live Spirit shows circa 1980/1981 - some from familiar recordings like The Agora, Cleveland 1981 or the Golden Bear, Huntington Beach 1980. Others - like the Uptown Theatre, Kansas City 1981 - are fresh to these ears. There aren't a lot of surprises here, with California's solo songs like 'Five In The Morning' and 'Shattered Dreams' sharing space with familiar Spirit songs like '1984'. But a couple of items do stand out - a previously-unreleased live reading of the rare Spirit song 'Give A Life, Take A Life' is delivered as a pastoral ballad, and this particular version of 'Hey Joe' was released in Germany as a 12" single.

Disc four reveals a few more treasures, including a strangely effective German version of 'Fearless Leader' (titled 'Grosser Herrscher'), replete with slippery synthesizer and an overall weird vibe. The unreleased 'His Spirit Is Traveling On' is a lofty spiritual ballad with vocals that float like gossamer above acoustic guitars, while 'PT109' is a somewhat tougher instrumental interlude with intricate guitar playing that segues nicely into the lovely 'Whispers From Heaven.' Half of disc four is from an October 1979 performance of The Randy California Band in Ayr, Scotland: with a roster that included bassist Steve 'Liberty' Loria and drummer Jack Willoughby.

If the first four discs haven't shriveled your eardrums into raisins, the last two discs will make your investment into the box set well worth the money. Disc five features a previously-unreleased Spirit concert from April 1981 in Greensboro, North Carolina. What the set lacks in sonic quality, it makes up for in energy, as California, Loria and Cassidy tear up a setlist leaning towards audience favorites like '1984,' 'Animal Zoo,' 'Mr. Skin,' 'I Got A Line On You' and covers like 'Wild Thing' and 'Like A Rolling Stone.'

The sixth and final disc features previously-lost 1982 performances of The Randy California Band at the Reading Festival in June, and the previously-mentioned Glastonbury Festival in August. California was joined by bassist Mike Sheppard and drummer Preston Hayman at both UK festival appearances. The Reading segment includes the entire 12-song performance sourced from the board tape, while the Glastonbury show is a soundboard recording of only five songs from the show, but they're all good. The Reading performance sounds a bit distant and hollow, but the delivery is powerful and hard rockin'. The Glastonbury tape sounds like it picked up halfway through the set, but it still includes a pair of cool unreleased tunes - the mid-tempo ballad 'Lisa,' and the punk-ish political diatribe 'Rebel On Attack,' along with tough-as-nails performances of the gun control anthem 'Hand Guns' and the eerie 'Killer Weed.'

Overall, there's enough meat on these six discs to make digging into this sparsely-documented portion of California's career, well worth your time.

Spirit Live Albums

For a band as dynamic, challenging, innovative and electrifying onstage as Spirit, one has to wonder why no live albums were released during their roughly six-year tenure with Ode/Epic Records, and three with Mercury. In the decades since, only one authorized live recording of the original Spirit has surfaced. This was *Live At The Ash Grove, 1967,* recorded by their friend Barry Hansen, and featuring summer rehearsals as the band was chasing its sound before signing with Lou Adler and Ode Records. It's hard to believe there isn't the odd live recording sitting in the Sony Music vault somewhere that could be dug up and released on vinyl for Record Store Day.

After leaving the relative comfort of their label deals, Spirit increasingly relied on live shows to pay the bills. Randy California recorded the shows on most nights, so it was inevitable that in later years there would be almost as many live album releases as there are Spirit studio albums. The live albums often included previously unreleased songs that may have been in the vaults for decades; the band taking their songs out on the road for a while before dropping them: making these rare performances much sought-after. Many of these late-period releases are also double sets, providing the Spirit fan with an abundance of live music.

Oddly enough, in spite of the hard-core Spirit fan's rabid enthusiasm, only a handful of unauthorized bootlegs have been released through the years. Robert Walker's 1992 book *Hot Wacks Book XV: The Last Wacks* only lists three such releases: *Live In Berlin* (Crash Records): a May 1981 performance; *1970 Live In Boston* (Flying Horses Records), and *Spirit From The Past* (no label listed), which includes 1966 demos and several live tracks from the 1978 *Rockpalast* TV show. In recent years, copyright-gap labels taking advantage of a loophole in the law, have taken notice of Spirit, and a few rare and engaging performances - like Ebbetts Field in 1974 and the Paramount Theatre in Seattle 1971 - have been released in various formats.

Live (1978)

Released on Miles Copeland's Illegal Records label, Spirit's first authorized live album has the three-piece power trio of California, Cassidy and bassist Larry 'Fuzzy' Knight. Pieced together from shows on the 1978 UK tour, it's a smorgasbord of sorts, of early and late-period Spirit material.

Album opener 'Looking Down' was never recorded for an album. This performance features Cassidy's subtle percussion, including what sounds like a Jew's harp in the background, along with California's imaginative fretwork, his extended solo leading into Knight's throbbing bass lines, and eliciting some audience applause.

'Animal Zoo' and 'Nature's Way' play fine sans former bandmate John Locke's keyboard skills - Cassidy substituting staccato rhythms in lieu of keys on the former; California providing jazz solos for the latter, while Knight's flanged bass, fills out both performances. California introduces '1984' by mentioning the song's *de facto* US radio ban. Cassidy's thundering rhythms lead into Knight's lofty vocal, Randy playing otherworldly licks appropriate to the futuristic theme. The unreleased 'Hollywood Dream' is an engaging rocker with vocal harmonies and busy rhythms driving California's wiry guitar; the time signature changing on a whim.

The band digs into *The Family That Plays Together* for 'It's All The Same', which opens with a squealing guitar before digging a deep groove. It's a largely percussive performance, Cassidy's hearty drum solos dominating, providing plenty of texture for spare guitar splashes. Jumping seamlessly into the same album's 'I Got A Line On You', this lack of keyboards is balanced somewhat by the scorching fretwork and a funky backbeat. The third previously-unreleased original song 'Downer' is a bluesy stomp-and-stammer rocker with Jimi-esque guitar licks and heaving bass lines, leading perfectly into a raucous cover of The Troggs' classic 'Wild Thing', to close the set.

Randy sweetened much of the record later in the studio (see the below entry for *Two Sides Of The Rainbow* for the entire story), but with live versions of three good-to-great unreleased songs, energetic performances, cool cover artwork and a decent sound for a low-budget recording, Spirit's *Live* is worth tracking down.

Live Spirit (1978)
With no introduction, Spirit leaps headfirst into 'Rock And Roll Planet' - a stout mid-tempo hard rock song built around 'Fuzzy' Knight's weighty bass lines, Cassidy's cymbal-heavy percussion, and high-flying California guitar solos. *Live Spirit* (not to be confused with the previous record) features the same three-piece power trio as its predecessor. Potato Records pieced it together from 1978 performances in the UK and Miami and Tampa, Florida.

After rocking everybody's socks off with a studio version of 'Rock And Roll Planet' complete with canned applause, comes the familiar 'Nature's Way' - this arrangement somewhat more-lofty and esoteric than on *Live*, displaying Spirit's penchant for changing things on the fly; no two performances exactly alike. The bass and drums are more prominent here, making for an interesting yin/yang dichotomy between the song's soft-psych roots and a harder rock sound. 'Animal Zoo' is approached differently, spacing out the chiming instrumental intro before the vocal kicks in; the middle of the song providing a canvas for extensive jamming before returning to the melody.

The strident vocal and fierce instrumentation of '1984' never cease to thrill, and this reading amps up the ambiance with a more nuanced performance featuring a big drum finish. A longer take of 'Looking Down' offers a breathtaking extended jam. There are also a couple of unreleased studio tracks - 'All The Same' and 'These Are Words' - both of which revolved in and out of setlists circa 1978/1979. The former is actually 'It's All The Same' from the *Live* album, but with more emphasis on the flamethrower guitar, and shorter drum solos. 'These Are Words' is a muscular mid-tempo hard rock number with gorgeous vocals and stunning guitar.

The setlist of *Live Spirit* is close to the previous *Live* LP, but there are many performance differences, possibly due to California's guitar overdubs. The cover art is atrocious (a grainy, unfocused live shot of Cassidy on the front, with similar band shots on the back), but the insert includes lyrics. The vinyl album has been replaced by the recent release of *Two Sides Of A Rainbow*.

Made In Germany (1983)

This title really has less to do with where the album was recorded and more with the country of origin, as this Potato Records release was *made* and released in Germany in cooperation with that country's Roof Records. There's one song from the *Rockpalast* TV show (more about that below), and the rest was sourced primarily from the band's Rainbow Theatre concert in the UK, and the aforementioned 1978 Florida performances used for *Live Spirit*. The 1993 CD reissue includes hard-to-decipher liner notes, poorly translated into English, with lyrics to match.

Night Of The Guitar Live! (1989)

Not exactly a Spirit LP as such, but included here because of Randy's participation. Night Of The Guitar Live was a fretboard-happy supershow dreamed up by I.R.S. Records founder Miles Copeland, who gathered some of the rowdiest guitar slingers he could find for seven UK gigs and a short European tour in late 1988. Alternating their time in the spotlight, talents like California, Steve Howe (Yes), Leslie West (Mountain), Robby Krieger (The Doors), Alvin Lee (Ten Years After), Pete Haycock (Climax Blues Band), Steve Hunter (Lou Reed/Alice Cooper) and Wishbone Ash's Andy Powell and Ted Turner, took turns showing off their chops for appreciative audiences.

A rock-solid band of bassist Derek Holt, drummer Clive Mayuyu (both from Haycock's solo outfit) and keyboardist Chris Bucknall, backed the guitarists, while Copeland served as master of ceremonies. In 1989, Copeland's I.R.S. subsidiary - the high-falutin' No Speak instrumental label - released the best performances as part of a double-vinyl set, including Randy's playing his song 'Groove Thing' with Haycock, and 'Hey Joe' by himself. Randy also participated in the show-closing take of Dylan's 'All Along The Watchtower,' which features most of the guitarists and Copeland's brother (and drummer for The Police) Stewart. Randy's energetic performances led to a one-off deal with I.R.S. Records for the release of *Rapture In The Chambers*.

An entertaining slice of Spirit ephemera, *Night Of The Guitar Live!* is something for the faithful, and inexpensive copies aren't hard to come by on the Discogs website.

Live At La Paloma (1995)

As Spirit's first live set released on CD, they take advantage of the extended playing time, include several *bonus* tracks. Unfortunately, they're mixed in with the main performance:an October 1993 show at the La Paloma Theater in

Encinitas, California. This makes for an uneven ride, sonically and stylistically. The extra tracks are derived from New York City shows in 1977 and 1981, 1987 (Detroit, MI), 1991 (Venice, CA) and 1993 (Auburn Hills, MI) - all of them varying in sound quality and intensity.

The main Encinitas show features Randy and Cassidy in their respective roles, along with keyboardist Scott Monahan, who also provides keyboard bass. It's an entirely new sound for the trio - a sort of new wave vibe that was cutting edge a decade earlier but had since been eclipsed by grunge, nerf metal and alternative rock. The sound quality is fairly good for an indie release, and the performance in front of what sounds like a sparse crowd is nevertheless engaged and electric.

Like most live Spirit sets of the era, *Live At La Paloma* includes a handful of previously-unreleased songs for which studio versions wouldn't surface until later. 'Sadana' is the most contemporary of these, evincing an unusual art-school vibe that echoes the alternative 1980s with its abundant keyboard riffs, but Randy's six-string creativity here is stunning. Another obscurity - 'Going Back To Jones' - is a little too funky for its own good, and the band can't pull it off. But 'Magic Wand' - from an April 1981 show at The Bottom Line in NYC (with Steve 'Liberty' Loria on bass) - is a rocker with choogling rhythms and razor-blade guitar licks. Then again, there's the somnambulant 'Living In This World': a treacly ballad that's one of the worst things California ever recorded.

Of the legacy material here, 'Life Has Just Begun' and 'Mr. Skin' benefit from Monahan's presence, and California sounds more alive than he had in years; his voice more confident than on earlier performances, coming into his own as a rock-'n'-roll singer. Several lengthy and mostly instrumental jams allow the band to stretch out and show their chops, and are period-appropriate for the 1990s - placing Spirit among fellow travelers like Phish, Dave Matthews Band and Blues Traveler (the H.O.R.D.E. Festival crowd). By no means essential, *Live At La Paloma* is nevertheless a lot of fun.

Live At The Rainbow Theatre 1978 (1999)
This dodgy UK release basically squeezes Spirit's two live 1978 albums onto a single CD, dropping a performance of 'Looking Down' from the latter album. The London-based Present & Past label was known for cutting corners and playing fast-and-loose with licensing, so I'm not exactly certain that California's estate authorized this release, and if you have the original vinyl records, there's nothing new to see here. If you're looking for these performances on CD, check out *Two Sides Of A Rainbow*: a legit two-disc set compiled by Mick Skidmore (see below).

Live From The Time Coast (2004)
One of the truly underrated gems in the Spirit catalog, *Live From The Time Coast* is a two-disc compilation of live performances of previously unreleased material, pieced together by Skidmore for the UK archival label Acadia Records.

Though drawn from a variety of sources dating from 1989 to 1996, and tape formats ranging from digital audiotape (DAT) and soundboard cassette recordings to professional-quality reel-to-reel tapes, Skidmore has done yeoman's work in equalizing the sound and cleaning it up as much as humanly possible. So while some performances are sonically weaker than others, there's no escaping the dynamism and electricity that Spirit could bring to the stage on a good night.

The 29-song tracklist is heavy on the late-1980s/early-1990s albums like *Rapture In The Chambers* and *Tent Of Miracles,* has a few Randy solo songs, and features rotating talents like Mike Nile, Scott Monahan and George Valuck playing alongside California and Cassidy. Skidmore's ability to stitch these performances into a nearly-seamless whole is impressive, as is the band's instrumental dexterity on rarely-captured songs like the stellar 'Golden Jam', which features both Nile's skillful bass-playing and Valuck's keyboards. It's a funky song that sounds like vintage Grateful Dead but with California's soaring fretwork out front.

In his extensive liner notes, Nile is quoted on playing behind California: 'He had nights where sometimes he was on automatic pilot. But some nights - like this one (in a small club in Germany), something happened, and all the glory days of guitar, all the struggle, screwed deals, great and lousy gigs, the pain and the joy, came out of that guy's guitar. Damn! He was brilliant!' That was the magic of Randy California, and the reason why his rabid fan base remains fiercely loyal to Spirit more than quarter of a century after the guitarist's tragic death. For all the live performances California captured on tape - even going so far as keeping a list on which he graded each (as Skidmore mentions in his liner notes) - only a handful have been found, and many of the remaining tapes aren't in the best physical shape.

As Spirit fans, we'll take pretty much whatever we can get, and *Live From The Time Coast* offers a tantalizing glimpse at California's talents in a live setting.

Salvation...The Spirit of 74 (2007)
This three-CD Acadia compilation flew under the radar when it was released, but it's worth another look. Comprised entirely of vintage 1970s live tracks, it has a bit of everything, including 18 tracks from the legendary Ebbets Field, Denver, Colorado performance in October 1974, five tracks from the November 1974 performance at the Agora Ballroom in Cleveland, Ohio, another three from a June-1975 show at the same venue, and three from the June-1975 show at the Armadillo World Headquarters in Austin, Texas. The sound quality varies wildly, from muddy lo-fi to marginally acceptable.

The Last Euro Tour (2010)
This now-out-of-print two-disc set compiled by Skidmore, documents the band's last European tour in 1991. Spirit at this time was California, Cassidy and bassist/vocalist Mike Nile. The setlist was an inspired mix of classics ('Fresh

Garbage,' 'Animal Zoo,' 'Mr. Skin,' 'I Got A Line On You'), covers ('Hey Joe,' 'All Along The Watchtower,' 'Wild Thing') and more-recent songs: a lot of them penned by Nile ('Tent Of Miracles,' 'Ship Of Fools,' 'Old Black Magic') for the *Tent Of Miracles* album. The sound quality is fairly dodgy and uneven, but there are 25 red-hot songs that benefit from California's then-renewed commitment to the Spirit ideal.

Rockpalast: West Coast Legends, Vol. 3 (2010)

In March 1978, California, Cassidy and Knight flew to Germany for a show scheduled to be broadcast on the legendary *Rockpalas*t TV show. First aired in 1974 and continuing to this day, *Rockpalast* (translated as Rock Palace) has broadcast performances from hundreds of rock, blues and jazz artists, reggae legends like Bob Marley and Black Uhuru, prog rockers like Camel and Spock's Beard, jazz-fusion bands like Weather Report, and rockers like Tom Petty and The Heartbreakers. On this night in Essen, Germany, Spirit held court for nearly two hours in front of an enthusiastic audience.

The show opens with the mighty Ed Cassidy pounding out a hybrid rock, blues and jazz solo that exhibits the best qualities of all three genres. Gradually, the other players glide in on a steely wind, the band freestyling the 'Rockpalast Jam' with a monster bass line courtesy of Knight, and the frontman's incendiary fretwork. Fully engaged with the *Rockpalast* crowd, Spirit cranks out a set of well-chosen covers and golden oldies, and these songs really *are* pure rock-'n'-roll gold mined from the Spirit catalog circa 1968-1970. Fan favorite 'Mr. Skin' suffers by lacking the original's lush, moody instrumentation and full-band harmonies, but the three-piece Spirit makes up for these shortcomings with amplification and audacity; California kicking up dust with the song's now-familiar solo, his use of sustain and feedback creating a glorious din.

The timeless 'Nature's Way' floats in with a mesmerizing blend of lofty vocal and ethereal instrumentation; the complex construction revealing itself in due time as California lets loose with a multicolored solo full of reckless energy and shimmering beauty. Spirit's biggest hit 'I Got A Line On You' is revved-up and rocked out with all the trappings you need - blast-beat drums, a humming bass line and the song's integral riff - familiar to any listener whose sense of rock-'n' roll history extends further back than the year 2000.

The broadcast closes with 'If I Miss This Train' - a bluesy guitar-driven number played with the assistance of Allman Brothers Band guitarist Dickey Betts, whose band Great Southern had performed earlier that night. At the time, *Rockpalast* was an open-ended broadcast - i.e., the show was over when the amps stopped buzzing - which allowed the producers to capture magical moments like this. California and Betts duel like a couple of grizzled gunfighters, the Spirit guitarist pursuing a tough-as-nails caked-in-mud sound, while Betts' sweet southern tone displays plenty of down-home twang and honey-covered soul.

Now out of print, *West Coast Legends* has been superseded by *Live At Rockpalast 1978*.

Tales From The Westside (2011)

The second of the Skidmore-curated live Spirit compilations follows up on the promises left by *Live From The Time Coast,* with two discs chock-full of 1990s Spirit performances featuring California, Cassidy and keyboardist Scott Monahan, who also wrote liner notes to go with Skidmore's comments. The sound quality is relatively uniform across these disparate performances, which date from circa 1993-1996, and from varying sources, with a couple of unknown venues thrown in for the fun of it.

The first four songs are a real treat - largely-acoustic November 1995 performances from Club Lingerie in Los Angeles that include bluesy treatments of traditionals like 'Jimmy Brown' and 'Dime For Beer' along with Randy's 'Cold Rainy Night.' Monahan sings his own 'Tales From The Westside,' bringing his soulful singing to a wistful, cinematic ballad. The rollicking '12,000 Miles' - which wasn't released in a studio version until 2005's *Son Of America* - features Randy's awe-inspiring solos. Monahan's 'Illusions' provides a fine showcase for California's underrated vocals, along with a slight raga feel. 'Hip Pretty Child' is another future *Son Of America* track - the song a throwback to Spirit's 1970s sound, with prog undertones and creative guitar/keyboard interplay.

There's also plenty of good stuff on disc two, including the usual songs like 'Nature's Way' and 'I Got A Line On You,' and an ambitious reinvention of 'Animal Zoo' as the hypnotic 'Zoo Jam' which largely eschews the song's original premise in favor of a free-form, improvised and entirely magical performance. California's freshly-written love ballad 'Love From The Heart' is built on gentle waterfalls of acoustic guitar. 'Cages' wears its spirituality on its sleeve - the lofty vocal and wiry fretwork combined with Monahan's vocal harmonies and spirited piano pounding. The seldom-visited 'Farther Along' opens with the sounds of industrial doom-and-gloom before pastoral acoustic-guitar picking chases the darkness away with rich, baroque elegance.

Two Sides Of A Rainbow (2012)

Here's where the story gets complicated, so we're going to go to Spirit archivist Mick Skidmore for information on this often-revisited concert that's central to the band's mythology. As he outlines in his extensive liner notes, the March 1978 show at The Rainbow Theatre in London was one of three UK Spirit shows and a fourth date in Essen, Germany, for the *Rockpalast* TV show. The Rainbow performance was taped for a live album. But, as Skidmore writes, 'As always, the credo with Spirit was, if something can go wrong, it will. And yes, it did.'

The guitar sound was missing from the tape, and Randy 'did indeed do no small amount of studio work to salvage the performance,' re-recording the missing parts for the *Live* album that Illegal Records later released. However, Skidmore continues, 'Randy - the perennial perfectionist - kept messing with the tapes, adding more and more overdubs.' He basically created versions of the same show that appeared on the *Made In Germany* and *Live Spirit* albums, with studio recordings of 'Rock And Roll Planet' and 'These Are Words' added with pre-recorded audience reactions.

Luckily, karma stepped in: 'Three decades after this memorable show, it was discovered that cassette tapes had been made of the board mix - i.e., what went on the board was what we got to hear at the show. Unfortunately, the tapes were of the absolute worst quality. But on the plus side, virtually all of the show was on the tapes, with all the guitar parts intact.' Luckily, Skidmore managed to salvage the entire two-hour performance, albeit not always with great sound quality. So what you have with the double-disc *Two Sides Of A Rainbow* is the definitive version of the legendary performance, warts and all, with half a dozen encore songs to soften the prospect of buying this show for a third (or fourth) time.

For the collector lacking some other version of this performance, the album is worth the investment. And for the Spirit fan, the opening track 'Rainbow Jam Electro Jam' is a six-minute master class in band chemistry and improvisation that will reel you in like a largemouth bass on the end of a hook. The aforementioned takes of well-worn songs like 'Nature's Way', 'Animal Zoo', '1984' and 'I Got A Line On You' benefit from the actual live performances, in spite of the buzzing, humming and poor sound quality, while previously-unreleased tracks like 'Like A Rolling Stone' have shimmering, reverent guitar hovering above Knight's intricate bass notes and Cassidy's cascading percussion.

Several encore songs that were absent from previous versions of the show, are where the magic takes flight. Taking up 35 minutes of the second disc, there are beautiful, otherworldly guitar sounds for the ethereal cover of 'All Along The Watchtower', which starts out slow, almost tentative, gradually building to an incredible climax of instrumentation and inspiration. *The Adventures Of Kaptain Kopter* album obscurity 'Turn To The Right' is a rambling, bluesy, droning song right out of R. L. Burnside's hill country blues songbook.

The band revisits the 'Rainbow Jam' with a short psychedelic reprise that leads into an explosive cover of Hendrix's 'Stone Free' that shows why the guitar innovator wanted the teenage Randy Wolfe in his band in the first place.

The US version of *Live Spirit* is on the second half of disc two, offering a stunning contrast between the organic original stage sounds of the first disc and the overdubbed and massively-restored 1978 masterwork.

At Ebbets Field (2015)

Due to loopholes in international law, so-called 'copyright gap' recordings have become a cottage industry for fly-by-night European Union companies releasing vintage radio broadcasts and other live recordings. As Bill Glahn writes on his The Original Live! Music Review website, 'They are officially registered companies in Europe, and use court interpretations of copyright law to legally manufacture unauthorized (by the artists) vinyl and CDs of broadcast recordings. These should never be considered sanctioned releases, only legal ones ... Although the radio and TV sources for these issues make for some good-to-excellent sounding albums, they are rarely - if ever - from master tape sources. Don't expect perfection.'

At Ebbets Field is one such CD, documenting an October 1974 show at the legendary (albeit small) Denver, Colorado venue Ebbets Field, and broadcast live on FM radio. This version - on the Good Ship Funke label - offers fairly decent sound for its vintage, and was likely sourced from a poor-quality station tape. (Lots of US FM radio stations are sitting on a goldmine of live-broadcast tapes of 1970s rock bands). The band lineup for the show includes California, Cassidy and original Spirit bassist Mark Andes, who was in between Jo Jo Gunne and Firefall.

The then-unreleased 'Love Will Open Your Door' is a subtle, slow-burning ballad that segues seamlessly into the more muscular 'Stormy Night' - Andes flexing his bass with Cassidy's drums while the psychedelic guitar solo flies around the room, before California jokingly introduces himself as Randy Colorado. His breathless vocal on 'America The Beautiful,' and lovely guitar lines, lead the listener into an earnest cover of Dylan's 'The Times They Are A-Changin' - the band weaving a mesmerizing tapestry of behind the voice.

Falling between albums (and record labels), *At Ebbets Field* is heavy with cover songs, but they're pretty good ones. California poorly singing 'Happy Birthday' to someone in the audience is slightly embarrassing, but the band's hard-as-nails reading of the Goffin/King gem 'I've Got To Use My Imagination' is a scorcher, with deep drum rhythms and bass lines as tough as a rhino hide. But it's Randy's roller-coaster fretwork that makes the song interesting. Dipping back into the Dylan songbook, 'All Along The Watchtower' is given an imaginative-if-familiar arrangement that relies heavily on six-string pyrotechnics (which bring Jimi's version to mind), before veering off in an entirely new and dangerous direction, aided and abetted by Andes' equally fluid bass work.

The reading of The Rolling Stones' '(I Can't Get No) Satisfaction' turns Keith Richards' legendary riff on its head - California vamping on vocals while tearing up his guitar with incendiary solos. Several of the original songs here showed up a year later on *Spirit Of '76*. Standouts include 'Veruska' (a knife-edged love song with switchblade guitars and tribal rhythms), and the gorgeous 'Sunrise': a throwback to the *Twelve Dreams* vibe and musical blueprint. Other songs only available on this album, are the whimsical and hypnotic 'Same Old Thing' (with strident vocals, quicksilver instrumentation and a surprising late-night gutter-jazz closing) and 'Better Run', which fuses a bluesy gospel delivery with jaunty percussion.

But even the legacy material here ('Nature's Way', 'I Got A Line On You') is enhanced with additional instrumental color and exciting new arrangements. While this particular CD is unauthorized, hard to find, and some of the songs have shown up on compilation albums (notably Mick Skidmore's *Salvation... The Spirit of '74*), it's one of Spirit's best shows - the trio holding court for a small-but-enthusiastic audience. It's also a showcase for several never-released songs, making it essential for the faithful.

Live At The Ash Grove, 1967, Volume 1 (2016)

In the beginning, the band that became known as Spirit were only steps away from their blues rock roots, heavily influenced by Rising Sons' Ry Cooder and Taj Mahal, and fellow travelers found at L.A.'s famed Ash Grove club. (A handbill from summer 1967 hypes shows by Big Mama Thornton, Ramblin' Jack Elliott, Sonny Terry and Brownie McGhee, and Spirits Rebellious). Randy's uncle Ed Pearl owned the club, and allowed the band to practice there on off-nights.

This album is a collection of those early proto-Spirit onstage rehearsals recorded by their friend and Ash Grove soundman Barry Hansen. It's also the only live recording of the original band. But due to its source and sound quality, it's a bit of a mixed bag. Archivist and producer Mick Skidmore had his work cut out for him baking and digitizing ten damaged reel-to-reel tapes, and though the sound is uneven (you can barely hear Cassidy's drums), it could be much worse considering the tape's neglect.

There are no real revelations among these dozen songs, which play Cassidy and Locke's free-jazz inclinations against the more bluesy California and Andes. There are a lot of instrumentals, which display the band's ready-made chemistry, and there's not really a lot for Jay Ferguson to do here. The band rolls through a handful of originals, like 'Free Spirit': a Wes Montgomery-style instrumental offering great guitar and keys interplay; 'Our Topanga Home' (which later evolved into the debut album's 'Topanga Windows') and 'Gramophone Man', which in its earliest incarnation skews closer to Captain Beefheart than *Dr. Sardonicus*.

The album includes some odd cover songs that didn't make the cut after the band evolved from Spirits Rebellious into Spirit - songs like an extended take on John Coltrane's 'Tunji,' California's first recording of the garage-rock gem 'Hey Joe' (which only get wilder and more-raucous through the years), and the traditional gospel standard 'Wade In The Water,' which is given a more bluesy treatment.

Overall, it's an interesting collection of live rehearsals, and shows where the band was creatively. But it's hardly essential.

Live At Paramount Theatre, Seattle, WA (2018)

Another unauthorized vinyl album issued on by DBQP Records, this offers part of a 1971 show broadcast live on Seattle's KISW-FM. The tracklist omits two songs from that night's set, but what it *does* include is pretty special! Randy's transcendent solos, pierce the murky sound quality; the recording largely mashing bass and keyboards together into a lumpy side dish, while Cassidy's drum sound is hit-and-miss - sometimes he noticeably blazes away, while on other songs, his contribution is all-but-lost in the dense mix. Whether it's

Ferguson or California at the microphone, their vocals are often hidden behind a wall of distortion and the echoey, cavernous nature of the poor, vintage recording.

Rare Spirit songs here, like the hippie ballad 'Going Away Somewhere' (which has some of Randy's most elegant and complex fretwork) or the psychedelic overkill and cheap thrills of 'Tow The Line,' more than make up for the cost of admission. The syncopated intro to 'Something You Must Say' features nuclear bass chords and powerful drums, leading into the intricately-woven guitar lines that ring clearly.

The obscure song 'Set Me Free' has plenty of guitar-hero gymnastics and pleading vocals as it builds to an instrumental crescendo. The now-requisite cover of 'Hey Joe' is slightly different from any other version - Randy expanding on how Jimi taught him to make every performance of it a devastating blues dirge, set alight by the juxtaposition of familiar chord structure against the in-the-moment improvisation.

So, what you have here is a vinyl bootleg with shabby sound quality. It's a rare recorded document of the entire original band, and a handful of songs are dynamite performances that appear nowhere else in the Spirit canon. What's not to love?

Live At Rockpalast 1978 (2019)

This is the same German TV performance that was released previously as *Rockpalast: West Coast Legends, Vol. 3.* But this three-disc set is even better, as it includes a DVD of the original TV broadcast, and two CDs comprising the entire show. So you get 16 red-hot songs instead of just 11! There's not a lot of Spirit video circulating, so this is a revelation.

Of the additional songs, 'Hollywood Dream' rocks like a scalded dog - the lyric inspired by the lives of these journeyman rockers. Knight's bass throbs like a jackhammer, Cassidy's Godzilla-sized rhythms echo like the voice of God, and California's raffish fretwork, rattles and buzzes like a jackknife comet. There's a lively 'Hey Joe' cover of the garage-rock classic, the trio bringing a dirtier sound, fatter bass and a barrage of drums. California doesn't mimic Jimi's electrifying original solo, as much as exaggerate it x 10, throwing in jazz licks and metallic riffs alongside the prerequisite blood, sweat and tears.

'Animal Zoo' is necessarily more sparse than the original, but the vocal flows effortlessly. Knight's bass plays the original second-guitar rhythm, and the song devolves into an improvised reprise of the 'Rockpalast Jam' before ending in an abrupt blurt. After 11 fine performances, the band leave the stage, only to return for an encore nearly half as long and every bit as energetic as the main show. This album is an essential addition to any Spirit collection.

Spirit Compilation Albums

Considering Spirit's glory years basically consisted of just four albums released between 1968 and 1970, the enduring quality of their innovative and complex music has led to an abundance of compilations seeking to draw in new fans and pacify the hard-core faithful. The commercial free-for-all that was the 1990s music biz, opened the door for a number of thoughtful and well-considered CD compilations (and later, again on vinyl), attracting an entirely new generation of Spirit fans.

Spirit (1973)

By 1973, Spirit had broken up - seemingly for good - so somebody at Epic Records decided to salvage what they could by releasing this two-LP set. Comprised of the eponymous debut album and the third record *Clear*, the set had nothing new for the faithful fan. Nevertheless, *Spirit* inched itself into the *Billboard* Top 200 at number 191. There was a pretty cool gatefold cover, however, with spacey lysergic-drenched front-and-rear photos reminiscent of *Twelve Dreams*, and informative liner notes by advertising guy Marty Pekar (who currently describes himself as a 'washed-up copywriter') who'd worked on CBS-Records campaigns for artists like Bob Dylan, and later for Elvis Costello. Sony reissued *Spirit* as a single CD in 1996.

The Best Of Spirit (1973)

The Best Of Spirit offers 11 tracks from the four Ode albums, including some of Spirit's best-loved songs. There's 'Fresh Garbage,' 'Mechanical World' and 'Uncle Jack' from the debut, while the following two albums are represented by 'I Got A Line On You' and 'Dark Eyed Woman.' The *Twelve Dreams* album does the heavy lifting with five songs, including 'Nature's Way' and 'Animal Zoo.' The outlier here is '1984', which was recorded after *Clear* was released, and wasn't on *Twelve Dreams*, which made *The Best Of Spirit* the only place to get it at the time. Subsequently supplanted by other compilations, this album has never seen a CD reissue.

Golden Spirit (1973)

A double vinyl set from Germany, this is in almost every way superior to the stateside *The Best Of Spirit*. First of all, it has a whopping 20 tracks, and not just the usual suspects, but lesser-known albeit worthy songs like the ten-minute jam 'Elijah', 'Jewish' and 'Drunkard' (*I Got A Line On You*), 'So Little Time To Fly' and 'Policeman's Ball' (*Clear*), the instrumentals 'Space Child' (*Twelve Dreams*) and 'Puesta del Scam' (*Feedback*), and the hard-to-find '1984' and 'Things Yet To Come' from California's *Kapt. Kopter* solo album. There's nothing fancy or rare here, but it's a well-thought-out effort.

Rock Giants (1982)

Another 'best of' compilation, this time from the Netherlands, and featuring what has to be the most generic album cover of all time. The edgy graphics overwhelm the much smaller band photo, and the back cover offers naught but a tracklist. CBS (Epic's parent company) basically took the debut album (omitting 'Elijah') and added 'Mr. Skin' and 'Animal Zoo' from *Twelve Dreams*. From a collectors' standpoint, you're better off getting the original releases.

Time Circle 1968-1972 (1991)

Back in 1991, CBS Records was bought by the Japanese conglomerate Sony Group, and was renamed Sony Music Entertainment (In 2004, Sony purchased CBS rival BMG: home of RCA Records). Digging through the vaults resulted in this double CD. At the time, only *Twelve Dreams Of Dr. Sardonicus* was available - the rest of Spirit's back catalog being out of print for over a decade.

The 41 tracks here include nine from the debut, seven from *The Family That Plays Together*, six from *Clear* and nine from *Twelve Dreams*. The rest of the tracks are unreleased songs, singles and B-sides, giving a crash course in Spirit's best. In his liner notes, Alan Robinson writes, 'There was no band quite like them back in the day, and there has never been anyone like 'em since. *Time Circle* is Spirit at their purest. Magical.'

Chronicles 1967-1992 (1992)

Released stateside by California's oddly-named independent W.E.R.C. C.R.E.W. label, this is a 22-track compilation designed to take advantage of Spirit's heightened profile following the previous year's *Time Circle*. Comprised largely of unreleased material, five songs are from the original 1967 demo tape produced by Barry Hansen (aka Dr. Demento). The musical building blocks for the future can be heard in these lo-fi tracks, from the imaginative riffing and vocal harmonies of 'If I Had A Woman' and the punk-folk reading of the rock chestnut 'Hey Joe,' to the alternative take of 'Elijah.' There are several live tracks, five 1991 re-recordings including 'Nature's Way' and 'So Little Time To Fly,' new songs like the brassy 'Stuck In L.A.,' and a cover of bluesman Mississippi Fred McDowell's 'Kokomo' featuring California's haunting circular riff. This album is a nice addition to the Spirit fan's collection, but I wish they'd given more background information on the recordings' origins.

The Mercury Years (1997)

This two-disc set culls material from the four mid-1970s Mercury albums, including a partial band reunion. Much of Spirit's original spark was gone by this time; the lineup changing from album to album but remaining anchored by California's guitar and Cassidy's drums.

Though the Mercury albums never matched the innovation and execution of the first four, there's still some good material here that has stood the test of time. California's Hendrix ode 'Sunrise' is a fitting tribute, while covers of 'Walkin' The Dog,' 'Like A Rolling Stone' and 'Hey Joe' offer new perspectives. The wonderful 'Green Back Dollar' - inspired by the assassination of John Lennon - is included as an unreleased bonus track.

Among the whopping 47 songs are almost all of the double *Spirit of '76,* nine
tracks from *Son Of Spirit*, 11 from *Farther Along,* and other odds and ends.
Though it was welcomed with open arms by Spirit fans - representing the first
CD of material from the band's middle period - the set has since been made
superfluous by Esoteric's 2021 *Sunrise & Salvation*: a monster eight-disc box
that wipes the Mercury vaults clean (see below).

Cosmic Smile (2000)
The beginning of what became a cottage industry comprised of many live and
studio recordings that Randy had stashed away over the years, *Cosmic Smile*
is the first posthumous compilation, and unsurprisingly it's a real gem! The
sound quality is reasonably even across the 15 tracks, with most of the music
jumping from the speakers with crystal clarity and plenty of instrumental
nuance. While most of the songs consist of Randy and his guitar, Ed Cassidy
appears on quite a few tracks, as do guitarist Matt Andes, his daughter Rachel,
journeyman drummer Bruce Gary and keyboardist Scott Monahan. Though the
album was compiled from various sources dating from 1991-1995, a certain
creative continuity runs through songs like 'Shake My Ego Down,' 'Barkin'
Up The Wrong Tree,' 'Mean And Beautiful' and the gorgeous 'Love From The
Heart' which was arranged by Jay Ferguson. Threaded throughout is Randy's
fluent and fluid guitar playing. And whether he's wielding a chiming acoustic
or a high-voltage electric guitar, his mastery of rock, blues and folk is amazing.
   Sadly, few Spirit fans got to hear *Cosmic Smile*, as Phoenix Gems only
released a handful of albums (including others by Southside Johnny and the
Asbury Jukes, The Tubes and Rick Derringer) before doing a disappearing act.
Luckily, CD copies are still relatively cheap and seemingly plentiful on Discogs.
Cosmic Smile features liner notes by music journalist Mick Skidmore, who
went on to play a much larger role for the band.

Eventide (2000)
This is the first of two collections of rarities, B-sides and outtakes. Archival
experts Sundazed Records released it on vinyl. The 11 songs lean towards the
band's jazz side. Recorded between 1968 and 1970, most tracks had already
appeared - as bonuses on Sony Legacy's 1996 CD reissues of Spirit's first four,
and, earlier, on *Time Circle*. There's really only one *new* recording here - the
unreleased 'Model Shop Rehearsal Theme 1' - and the two radio spots that
close side two. Still, producer and Sundazed head Bob Irwin put together an
impressive package, with song-by-song commentary from Cassidy, Ferguson,
Andes and Locke.
   In his *All Music* review, William Ruhlmann wrote: 'Like its companion
volume *Now or Anywhere*, *Eventide* will be more of an artifact for Spirit fans
than a necessary release, particularly since so much of the material is also
available digitally. But it will make a nice complement to those scratchy old
LPs for vinyl fans.'

Now Or Anywhere (2000)

The second Sundazed compilation offers eight tracks from 1967 and 1968 that all saw earlier release on *Time Circle* (Sundazed's Irwin was that compilation's producer) or as bonus tracks on the Sony Legacy 1996 CD reissues of *Spirit* and *The Family That Plays Together*. Licensing the material for release on vinyl only (Vinyl wasn't even on the major-label radar in 2000), Irwin leans towards Spirit's more-jazz alter ego, and songs like 'Free Spirit' and 'Mellow Fellow' reflect songwriter/keyboardist Jon Locke's deep musical roots and composition skills. The second alternative take of 'Elijah' is just as breathtaking as the original, and an early version of 'Space Chile' showcases the song's evolution.

Like its predecessor, this album includes song-by-song band commentary. *Eventide* and *Now Or Anywhere* are a joyful document of Spirit's early years.

The Very Best Of Spirit - 100% Proof (2000)

This turn-of-the-century European compilation doesn't stray far from previous Spirit collections. Nevertheless, it's a curious amalgam of Ode/Epic Records-era tracks (i.e., 'Fresh Garbage,' 'Mr. Skin,' 'Animal Zoo,' 'I Got A Line On You'), with a handful of songs from *Kapt. Kopter* ('Day Tripper,' 'Mother And Child Reunion,' 'Walkin' The Dog'), the ill-fated *Potato Land* ('Turn To The Right') and Mercury material. It may be a little more adventurous than usual for Sony, but it's unnecessary if you have all of those original records.

Sea Dream (2002)

Mick Skidmore moves up to producer status, digging up 28 unreleased tracks from Randy's hoard, for this two-disc collection released by Acadia Records in the UK. You get over two hours of new music: much of it in a slightly different vein than your usual Spirit jams. Skidmore explains the differences in his comprehensive liner notes:

> In many ways, Randy was a deeply spiritual and sensitive human being. He - like many of us - looked for a better understanding of the world and our place in it … The elements of India certainly seem to be prevalent in much of the material on this disc. Randy made several trips to India to study the teachings of Sai Baba. Many of the songs on this disc reflect Randy's feelings for those spiritual teachings. The music may be stylistically very different from much of Randy and Spirit's other work, but there's a sense of comfort, peace and tranquility in it.

Therefore, much of *Sea Dream* is loftier but instrumentally lighter than Spirit's usual rockin' fare, with a slight exotic tilt. Some standout tracks ('Jack Rabbit' comes to mind) pursue a hard-edged prog-rock sound, not unlike early Genesis or Jade Warrior. Though Randy plays guitar, bass, percussion and keyboards, Ed Cassidy and Scott Monahan feature on many tracks. Disc two includes the eight-song 'Sea Dream Suite', which California had been slowly and deliberately composing since the mid-1980s with the goal of eventually releasing it as an album. Mostly instrumental, the title suite alone is worth the price of admission.

If you've read this far in the book, you're going to want copies of all three of the Skidmore-curated Acadia compilations, which not only shine well-deserved light on California's immense talents, but also provide the hard-core Spirit fan with over six hours of new music. The compilations are reasonably easy to find online.

Blues From The Soul (2003)

The second of the Skidmore Acadia compilations, these two discs set are primarily a blues and folk-oriented set of originals and classic cover songs that California planned on releasing as an album at some point. Working with musicians like stepdad Ed, bassist Steve 'Liberty' Loria, keyboardist Scott Monahan and slide guitarist Matt Andes, Randy rips and roars through blues standards like Blind Willie Johnson's 'Gonna Need Somebody On Your Bond,' Big Bill Broonzy's 'Key To The Highway' and Wilbert Harrison's R&B hit 'Kansas City.' The original tracks ain't half bad either - 'Wagon Of Wood' features Andes' serpentine slide work, while 'Tell Me (Didn't Mean No Harm To You)' is a smooth, jaunty blues jam with smoky vocals and jazz licks.

Sadly, Randy shelved the original album, though revisited the concept a couple of years later with the brilliant *California Blues*, which shares several of these songs. Some of this material was included on 2000's *Cosmic Smile* CD, but as virtually nobody bought that album, Skidmore tacked them onto this set because they deserved to be heard.

Disc two was compiled of tracks from various period DATs, including a couple of dynamite covers like Randy's scorching take on The Box Tops' hit 'The Letter', Willie Dixon's blues standard 'Ain't Superstitious' and various outtakes and demos, which all do a solid job of exploring where California was headed at the time.

Between *Sea Dream* and *Blues From The Soul*, one thing is glaringly obvious: Randy California was writing and recording an astounding amount of material in the early-1990s. Skidmore wrote in the album liner notes: 'The early-to-mid '90s - where most of this material stems from - were tough times for this uncompromising but compassionate individual and his band. The major labels had sadly lost interest in the music of Spirit and Randy California. Gigs were less frequent than core members California and Cassidy would have liked. Nonetheless, in the face of adversity, the band went into a surprisingly creative period.'

An Introduction To Spirit (2004)

These 23 tracks were compiled by UK music magazine *Mojo* and given away as a cover-mounted CD. Drawing from the first four Ode/Epic albums, there's a lot of the usual fare, but the magazine's Johnny Black provides extensive and informative liner notes, and there are a handful of rare photos. Considering it had been more than ten years since *Time Circle* and eight since the CD reissues of the first four, the time was right to remind people of Spirit's special sound. *Mojo* editor and chief Phil Alexander wrote an apt introduction: 'From jazz, blues, folk and on to granite-hard rock, such is Spirit's assimilation and translation of influences, that by rights they should be name-checked alongside fellow American adventurers The Beach Boys, The Doors and The Byrds.'

Son Of America (2005)

The third of the initial Acadia/Skidmore trilogy is a deep dive into the archives. It came hot on the heels of the impressive *Live From The Time Coast* collection. The two CDs offer a whopping 44 songs, clocking in at nearly 160 minutes. It's an exhaustive but satisfying listening experience. Faced with the daunting task of compiling his fourth double-disc set in a mere four years (including Live From The Time Coast), Skidmore took a different tack, writing in his liner notes:

> This latest trawl through the Randy California/Spirit archives, concentrates on unreleased studio material that puts more of an emphasis on Randy's songwriting abilities. There are strong sociopolitical tones to many of the songs, as well as familiar themes that explore love, spirituality and self-awareness. All are immersed in that inimitable melodic style that Randy was so good at. As the material used here spans over a decade, I've attempted to not only present music that was stylistically compatible, but I've tried to thematically link them by using various instrumental interludes and jams as segues.

This is an entertaining and nearly seamless collection that's as authentic a Spirit album as anything since *Spirit Of '76*. From the trippy instrumental 'Space Jam' to the hauntingly beautiful '20 Years' and the fierce, spacey 'Gyrations Of War,' these recordings capture California at his most creative and experimental, soldiering on in the face of industry indifference, because his hyperactive and over-amped muse was a force of nature that couldn't stay quiet.

The Archive... An Introduction (2008)

Acadia revisits Spirit with this introductory 20-track compilation that (unlike most of these compilations) focuses on the band's late-period independent releases. Three songs are from *Son Of America*, five from *Sea Dreams*, four from *Blues From The Soul*, two from *Live From The Time Coast*, and the rest from the *Salvation...The Spirit of '74* and *The Euro-American Years* box sets.

Rock And Roll Planet... 1977-1979 (2009)

Another ambitious three-disc Acadia set compiled by Mick Skidmore. The first two discs document Los Angeles, New York City and Texas shows from between 1977 and 1979. Disc three has 18 studio tracks - mostly outtakes from the late-

1970s - and closes with eight California solo acoustic tracks. The sound quality is pretty dodgy - the source recordings often stereo tapes or cassettes. This album is not recommended, especially if you already have most of Spirit's live 1980s albums.

Fresh From The Time Coast: The Best of 1968-1977 (2009)

This fairly comprehensive two-CD Australian compilation offers an inspired mix of Ode/Epic recordings alongside songs from the Mercury releases, and even throws in a couple of *Kapt. Kopter* tracks. It's nowhere near a necessity.

The Original Potato Land (2011)

Epic Records shelved California's ill-fated second solo album. But Rhino Records released a largely re-recorded version of *The Adventures of Kaptain Kopter & Commander Cassidy In Potato Land* in 1981. This 2011 Retroworld two-disc set is the latest iteration of the concept album, which you read about at length in a previous chapter. Mick Skidmore sourced it from a BBC radio broadcast of an acetate. This set has been expanded with bonus tracks, bootleg-quality live performances, and studio outtakes that further explain Randy's humorous social commentary and satirical intent.

Shorn of the previous release's overdubs and re-recordings, this is the definitive version of the original vision for the *Potato Land* album. There's some pretty cool stuff here for the hard-core fan, like the re-imagined versions of '1984' and 'Nature's Way,' the ethereal 'Lonely In Potato Land (Mashed Potatoes)' and the psych-sopped 'Salvation: Matter Of Time: Suite.' Disc one includes a California and Cassidy interview with BBC radio DJ Bob Harris. Skidmore wrote in the CD liner notes: 'Hopefully this release, despite some sonic flaws, finally puts the concept in proper context', concluding that it 'fills in something of a missing link in the music of Randy California and Spirit.'

In his *Shindig! Quarterly* review critic Mike Fornatale wrote, 'Musically there's no contesting that this was the next logical step - as well as the next chronological one - after *Dr. Sardonicus*, and that ought to be enough endorsement right there. This may be a rough ride if you're not an uber-fan, but ultimately well worth it.'

It Shall Be: The Ode & Epic Recordings 1968-1972 (2018)

UK archive label Esoteric Recordings has done a stellar job in preserving and restoring Spirit's immense musical legacy, starting with this comprehensive five-CD 2018 clamshell box set of remasters. Among the rarities are the mono mix of the debut *Spirit* (here on CD for the first time), the original stereo mix of *The Family That Plays Together*, the complete *The Model Shop* film soundtrack and a slew of outtakes, singles and alternative mixes exclusive to the 1991 *Time Circle* compilation. The box also includes an illustrated booklet with liner notes by writer Malcolm Dome, and archive interviews with California and Cassidy. For the newcomer to Spirit, *It Shall Be* provides much of what you need to know about the band. Additional study can be completed with the below-listed Esoteric box set *Sunrise & Salvation*.

Sunrise & Salvation: The Mercury Era Anthology (2021)

Esoteric Recordings went above and beyond with this huge eight-CD clamshell box set ostensibly collecting every note Randy and Spirit ever recorded for Mercury Records between 1975 and 1977. The first disc includes most of the *Spirit Of '76* album - a double LP that runs over to this set's second disc - which is then rounded out by 14 alternate and live tracks, including performances of 'Nature's Way,' 'Mr. Skin,' 'Fresh Garbage' and a rowdy cover of The Rolling Stones' 'Happy' - all taken from a November 1974 show in Cleveland, Ohio: some of which was released on *Salvation*.

Disc three includes the *Son Of Spirit* and *Farther Along* albums and a handful of studio outtakes, while disc four includes all 22 songs from *Future Games* (the re-tagged Randy *solo* album with just him and drummer Cassidy) and almost a dozen unreleased outtakes and demos from 1976 and 1977. Things get really interesting by disc five, which offers the rare *reunion* album *The Thirteenth Dream* and six previously-unreleased live tracks from a 1986 Detroit, Michigan show.

Disc six is titled Spirit of Salvation, and includes 1974/1975 studio material released in 2007 as part of *Salvation...The Spirit of 74*, along with eight Randy demos. Disc seven offers more of the 1975 Spirit show at the Armadillo World Headquarters in Austin, Texas (the venue long since torn down and replaced by an office building).

The final disc - eight- closes with early demos of *Future Games* songs and an eight-song live performance from The Agora in Cleveland in June 1975. The set features Mick Skidmore's extensive liner notes and a lot of rare band photos: pretty much making it a no-brainer purchase for the dedicated fan.

Spirit vs. Led Zeppelin

In late 1968 and early 1969, a little-known British blues-rock band named Led Zeppelin toured as openers for the major-label group Spirit. Zeppelin guitarist Jimmy Page - at the time a well-respected session musician and former member of popular 1960s UK band The Yardbirds - was intrigued with the Spirit songs 'Taurus' and 'Fresh Garbage,' later performing both songs onstage with Zeppelin. Page later *borrowed* (allegedly) the opening guitar arpeggio from 'Taurus' for the acoustic intro to Zeppelin's incredibly successful 1971 song 'Stairway To Heaven' from their landmark untitled fourth album, typically referred to as *Led Zeppelin IV*.

Flash-forward a few decades to May 2014, when former Spirit bassist Mark Andes and representatives for the Randy C. Wolfe Trust filed a copyright infringement suit against Led Zeppelin and requested an injunction against the planned *Led Zeppelin IV* CD reissue. Claims were also made for contributory copyright infringement, vicarious copyright infringement and equitable relief in the form of granting 'Taurus' songwriter Randy California a right of attribution as composer on 'Stairway To Heaven.' Requesting a jury trial in the case, the plaintiffs asked for a third of the song's royalties, which at the time were estimated to be in excess of $550,000,000 USD.

Naturally, Led Zeppelin fought back: first, with a motion to dismiss the suit altogether. But in April 2016, Los Angeles District Judge Gary Klausner ruled that there were enough similarities between 'Stairway To Heaven' and 'Taurus' for a jury to settle the claim. On 23 June 2016, the jury ruled that the songs' similarities did not amount to copyright infringement. The Randy C. Wolfe Trust appealed the decision, arguing that the jury should've been allowed to hear a recorded version of 'Taurus'. The appeal wove its way through the notoriously sluggish US court system, and in September 2018, a three-judge panel of the Ninth Circuit US District Court ordered a new trial based on evidentiary and procedural issues. The case was heard by the full appeals court in September 2019. In March 2020, the judges upheld the original jury finding, ruling that there should be no new trial to determine plagiarism. Further plaintiff appeals to the US Supreme Court were denied, thereby settling the controversy, at least in a legal sense.

Without getting too deep into legalese, the basic argument was that due to an oversight in the law, sound recordings created before 1978 were not protected by copyright. The judges declared that the scope of copyright for both songs lay not in the recorded version, but in the 'deposit copy' of their sheet music registered with the US copyright office. Because the copyright office could not produce a 'deposit copy' of Spirit's 'Taurus' for the trial, there was no proof of copying. Zeppelin's lawyers additionally argued that evidence of the band's access to 'Taurus' was speculative and inadmissible - and besides, Page claimed he hadn't even heard 'Taurus' until 2014, and that the song was a 'work for hire' anyway: meaning the Wolfe estate didn't own the song's publishing and didn't have standing for an infringement lawsuit. Page's claims

of ignorance notwithstanding (It's unlikely he hadn't heard 'Taurus' until that
late date), his argument that the similarity between the two songs was 'limited
to a descending chromatic scale of pitches', and that the two songs bore no
likeness in harmony or melody beyond that descending scale, is a valid one.
The musicologist hired by the plaintiffs couldn't produce evidence of striking
similarities between the two songs beyond the short instrumental introduction.

The decision, in this case, could end up having long-term implications for how
copyright law is applied to recorded material. The Ninth Circuit used its decision
to overturn the controversial 'inverse ratio rule' that courts had relied on in
copyright rulings for decades. The rule basically holds that the more access an
alleged infringer had to a work, the lower the threshold for establishing essential
similarity. The appeals court noted that the rule 'is not part of the copyright
statute, defies logic, and creates uncertainty for the courts and the parties,'
thereby overturning its 1977 ruling. The decision opened the door for other
defendants in copyright infringement cases to appeal negative decisions.

Regardless of where you stand on the Spirit vs. Led Zeppelin controversy,
the fact remains that 'Stairway To Heaven' used less than a minute of 'Taurus'
as an acoustic introduction to what is otherwise an eight-minute song. Yes, it's
my personal belief that consciously or not, Page picked up on that descending
'Taurus' and incorporated it into 'Stairway' along with a bunch of other
elements. Musicians pick up scraps of music and lyrics from each other all the
time, and blues music was built on new rewrites of traditional songs.

But Led Zeppelin have a lengthy and contentious history of *borrowing* from
other artists - sometimes wholesale, and often without attribution, making
the band easy targets. A 2010 lawsuit against Zeppelin by folk songwriter Jake
Holmes over the *Led Zeppelin I* song 'Dazed And Confused' was settled out
of court, with Holmes' name added to the songwriting credit alongside Page.
Willie Dixon sued the band over their use of lyrics from his song 'You Need
Love' in their *Led Zeppelin II* song 'Whole Lotta Love.' This was also settled
without trial, as was their appropriation of the Chester Burnett's (aka Howlin'
Wolf) song 'Killing Floor' in creating 'The Lemon Song.' Other Zeppelin
songs were allegedly borrowed freely from material written by Bob Mosley of
Moby Grape, Ritchie Valens, Bert Jansch, and bluesmen Bukka White, Robert
Johnson, Sleepy John Estes and Blind Willie Johnson.

In the liner notes to the 1996 *Spirit* CD reissue, Randy wrote, 'People always
ask me why 'Stairway To Heaven' sounds exactly like 'Taurus,' which was
released two years earlier. I know Led Zeppelin also played 'Fresh Garbage' in
their live set. They opened up for us on their first American tour.' Writer Will
Shade elaborated upon this in his 2001 article for *Perfect Sound Forever* (which
Shade updated in 2008):

There is no doubt that Page appropriated the opening guitar lines note-for-note
on 'Stairway To Heaven.' Further, the chord progression in 'Stairway To Heaven' is
incredibly similar to a song by the Chocolate Watch Band: 'And She's Lonely.' The

Yardbirds played with The Chocolate Watch Band during Page's tenure. It would be quite ironic if he did indeed lift the chords from The Chocolate Watch Band. The Chocolate Watch Band - to those in the know - were the ultimate Yardbirds clone. Wouldn't it be fitting that a former Yardbirds guitarist ripped off something from a band that based an entire career around sounding like that famed quintet?

There's no doubt California recognized the similarity between the two songs, and shrugged his shoulders rather than file a lawsuit. In a December 2021 interview with *Mojo* magazine, Jimmy Page told writer Mark Blake: 'Anyone who knows *anything* about playing guitar, knows some things have been around forever. I wanted to go into court with my guitar and show the difference, but I wasn't allowed to.'

In a 2021 *Shindig!* magazine interview with Thomas Patterson, British rock legend Nick Lowe had perhaps the last word on songwriters borrowing from one another:

When you get an idea for a song, and you start trying to bring it on, you put in a pinch of everything you've stolen from everyone, and then it's not stolen anymore - it becomes your own special sauce of stuff that you've absorbed over the years. That's how you get your own style. Everything's been done. There's nothing new under the sun - pop has been eating itself for at least 50 years. So anyone who thinks they're creating something new, is very much mistaken.

Life Before And After Spirit
Randy California

Sadly, for Randy California, there would be no life after Spirit. The guitarist and his stepfather Ed struggled to keep the band's dream alive through the 1990s. Then tragedy struck - on 2 January 1997, Randy drowned in the Pacific Ocean while rescuing his 12-year-old son from a riptide near his mother's home in Molokai, Hawaii. Randy pushed his son to safety, but succumbed to the current himself. His body was never found.

Through the years, Randy California's musical legacy has only grown. His extraordinary talent continues to attract new fans 25 years later. The Randy Craig Wolfe Trust - formed after his death and funded by his royalties - supports the Randy California Project: an after-school education program for underprivileged students in Ventura County, California.

Ed Cassidy

Unlike Randy (to whom Ed was musically joined at the hip for decades), there was some semblance of 'life after Spirit' for drummer Ed Cassidy. His striking visage - shaved head, dressed in black, and years older than his bandmates - earned him the nickname Mr. Skin, and he was as big a part of Spirit's rock-'n'-roll image as were Jay Ferguson and Randy California. Cassidy was the only Spirit member to play with every version of the band - his unique, jazz-flecked drum sound appearing on almost 20 albums over 30 years.

After Randy's death, Cassidy performed for over a decade with psych-surf artist Merrell Fankhauser in The Fankhauser Cassidy Band, recording several albums and making videos for Fankhauser's *Tiki Lounge* cable TV show. Cassidy played drums until nearly his death, earning him a listing in the *Guinness Book of World Records* as the world's oldest performing rock-'n'-roll drummer. He also had numerous interests outside of music, working as an actor (including live improvisation) and studying and writing about history. From his Southern California home, he corresponded with fans until his death from cancer on 6 December 2012 at the age of 89.

In 1991, Cassidy told the Los Angeles Times, 'Rock-'n'-roll music really saved my bacon musically. What I wanted was a band with no categories, that could attempt anything, any style, and make it their own.' This was later quoted in Cassidy's *Los Angeles Times* obituary.

John Locke

The erstwhile keyboardist probably has the most sparse post-Spirit CV of the core members. Leaving the band in the late-1970s after the Mercury era, Locke hooked up with Scottish hard rock band Nazareth circa 1980/1982 - appearing on *The Fool Circle* (1980), *2XS* (1982) and the live *'Snaz* (1981). Locke also lent his considerable keyboard skills to The Stray Cats' 1981 album *Gonna Ball*. Despite his differences with Randy California, Locke appeared on Randy's *Euro-American* and *Restless*, and on late-period Spirit recordings like

The Thirteenth Dream and *Rapture In The Chambers*. Largely retiring from performing in the 1990s, Locke settled in the Ventura County, California tourist destination of Ojai, where he ran a small recording studio until his death from cancer on 4 August 2006 at the age of 62.

Mark Andes

In contrast to some of his former bandmates, bassist Andes has enjoyed a significant post-Spirit career. A high school friend of Jay Ferguson, Andes was an early member of the blues-rock band Canned Heat as a teenager, playing with them for a couple of months, but leaving before they signed their Liberty Records deal. He returned to The Red Roosters just before they changed their name to Spirits Rebellious, and, later, to Spirit. After recording four albums with Spirit, Andes went with Ferguson to form Jo Jo Gunne, bringing in his brother Matt on guitar. Andes recorded only one album with Jo Jo Gunne, enjoying a top-40 hit with 'Run, Run, Run' before retiring from music in 1972. (Andes was part of the 2004 Jo Jo Gunne reformation, releasing the album *Big Chain* in 2005.)

Andes' 1972 retirement didn't last - after leaving Jo Jo Gunne, he ended up in Boulder, Colorado, where former Flying Burrito Brothers member enlisted Andes to form the country-rock outfit Firefall with former Byrds drummer Michael Clarke. Andes spent six years with Firefall, playing on four albums as the band reeled out a string of hit singles through to the end of the 1970s: including the top-10 hit 'You Are The Woman.' Andes left Firefall after their 1980 album *Undertow*, returning to California and working as a session musician.

A couple of years later, Ann and Nancy Wilson recruited Andes to join Heart, and he played on their 1983 album *Passionworks*. He stayed with Heart for ten years, playing on three top-10 Heart albums, including their chart-topping 1985 self-titled album, and seven top 10 singles, including 'What About Love', 'Alone' and 'Nothin' At All.' After Heart, Andes returned to session work, playing with artists as varied as Joe Walsh, Alejandro Escovedo, Ian McLagan and The Bump Band, Brian Auger, and his old Spirit bandmate Jay Ferguson, among others.

Andes released his only solo album *Real World Magic,* in 2009. Through the years, he frequently reunited with California and Cassidy, appearing on late-period Spirit albums like *The Thirteenth Dream* (aka *Spirit of '84*) and *Rapture In The Chambers*. In 2014, Andes began playing with the reunited Firefall, where he remains to this day.

Jay Ferguson

Singer-songwriter Jay Ferguson took a different career path after leaving Spirit, first forming Jo Jo Gunne with the Andes brothers. Named after a 1958 Chuck Berry single, Jo Jo Gunne originally included guitarist Matt Andes and drummer William 'Curley' Smith. Ferguson wrote and sung virtually all of the band's songs, and they spent several years touring in support of albums like *Bite Down Hard* (1973), *Jumpin' The Gunne* (1974) and *So...Where's The*

Show? (1975), but they never followed up on the initial success of the hit single 'Run, Run, Run' and their self-titled debut album.

Creem magazine critic Gerrit Graham wrote the following in his review of Jo Jo Gunne's *Bite Down Hard*:

> Spirit - one of the most interesting and musically superior of American bands - seems finally to have croaked for good. Randy California went off to waste his fecund imagination on Sgt. Twirly and His Wonderful Birdfuckers, or whatever that mess of self-indulgent cowflop was called, leaving John Locke and the chrome-dome drummer to the Staehely brothers and the vapid *Feedback*. But what of Mark Andes and Jay Ferguson? Well, they put together Jo Jo Gunne, petitioned the shade of Moby Grape for guidance, and came up with one of the nicest rock-and-roll records of last year ... If you preferred Spirit at their hardest; if you pine for the great Grape, you'll like it a lot. Jo Jo Gunne rocks out righteously, and that about covers it.

After Jo Jo Gunne fell completely apart (Mark Andes bolted after the first album, his brother Matt after the third (eventually replaced by former Spirit guitarist John Staehely), Ferguson took more than a year off to regroup. Superstar producer Bill Szymczyk convinced Ferguson to visit him at his Coconut Grove Recording Studio in Miami, where he was working on Joe Walsh's *You Can't Argue With A Sick Mind* album. Ferguson played piano and sang backing vocals on the record, and Szymczyk helped him get a solo deal with Asylum Records.

Ferguson recorded three albums for Asylum - *All Alone In The End Zone* (1976), *Thunder Island* (1977) and *Real Life Ain't This Way* (1978) - scoring a top-10 hit with his second album's title track, and nearly making the top-30 with the single 'Shakedown Cruise', from his third Asylum album. With his contract fulfilled, Ferguson jumped to Capitol Records, releasing two albums - *Terms and Conditions* (1980) and *White Noise* (1982) - which performed only modestly in a marketplace dominated by new wave and hard rock.

During this time, Ferguson reunited with Spirit for *The Thirteenth Dream*, and also sang on California's *Euro-American* album. In this period, Ferguson also did a fair amount of session work as a singer and keyboardist on further albums by Joe Walsh, Gary Myrick, John Mellencamp, Keith Moon and Crosby, Stills and Nash, among others.

Deciding that enjoyed composing more than the constant grind of touring, Ferguson became a soundtrack composer for movies and television, finding a great deal of success. He has written music for over 15 feature films, including *A Nightmare On Elm Street 5: The Dream Child* and *Gleaming The Cube*. But he's become best known as a TV composer, contributing to shows like *Melrose Place* and *Tales From The Crypt*. He won the 2007 Film & TV Music Award for Best Score for a Comedy Television Program for his theme to the American version of *The Office*, and he has composed for the popular *NCIS: Los Angeles* TV show since 2010.

Other Members of the Spirit Family
Al Staehely

A contentious figure among the faithful, singer-songwriter and bassist Al Staehely helped keep the Spirit name alive at a time when Randy was recuperating and unable to tour. Al's version of Spirit with his brother John on guitar and founders John Locke and Ed Cassidy, recorded 1972's controversial *Feedback*, and toured extensively in support of the album. That California and Cassidy let the Staehely brothers walk off with the Spirit name and had to later buy it back, has more to do with their oversight than with Al's keen knowledge of the law (see below).

When Cassidy and Locke split from the band, Al and John recorded the 1973 album *Sta-Hay-Lee* for Epic Records under the Staehely Brothers name. In 1982, Polydor released Al's solo album *Stahaley's Comet* (sic) in Europe, and he toured and recorded sporadically with Nick Gravenites and John Cipollina, appearing on their 1982 album *Monkey Medicine*. More recently, Staehely has performed with his band The Explosives, releasing the *Cadillac Cowboys* EP in 2013 on the Austin indie label SteadyBoy Records. Staehely has also found some success as a songwriter, with material recorded by artists as diverse as Bobbie Gentry, Keith Moon (The Who), Marty Balin (Jefferson Airplane/Starship), and his bandmates Gravenites and Cipollina.

Staehely always had a backup plan in case the rock-'n'-roll life didn't pan out, as he'd graduated with his JD degree from the University of Texas Law School in 1970 and was admitted to the Texas bar before moving to Los Angeles. He's been a practicing entertainment attorney for the music and film industries since 1979, working with musicians, record labels, publishing and film production companies. Staehely has also taught music publishing and music business law at the Art Institute of Houston and St. Thomas University in Houston - his firsthand experience no doubt providing valuable insight. He is also a member of The National Academy of Recording Arts and Sciences. In an interview accompanying his biography on the Music Lawyer website, Staehely states, 'Law didn't lead me to music. Music delivered me to law. Like so many others, I played in bands while in high school (Austin, Texas), in university (The University of Texas) and in law school (The University of Texas School of Law). Unlike most others, I didn't practice law for almost ten years after graduating. I joined the group Spirit, wrote songs, recorded for Epic records and toured the world.'

Larry 'Fuzzy' Knight

Born to a middle-class Jewish family (his given name is 'Weisberg') in St. Louis in 1944, young Larry was a child prodigy, learning to play violin, cello and upright bass at an early age. By the time he was a teen, he was reading and writing music, and had a bright future as a composer were it not for fate intervening. Listening to the *all-black* radio station in St. Louis, Knight fell in love with R&B - an obsession cemented after seeing shows by legends like Otis Redding, Ray Charles and James Brown. At 16, Knight went across the bridge to East St. Louis, and jammed with talents like Chuck Berry, Albert King and Ike

Turner. In 1966 he led his own band Larry Knight and The Upsetters, scoring a regional hit with 'Hurt Me.'

However, Vietnam was calling; the war threatening to derail Knight's promising musical career when he was drafted into service. After his 1968 discharge, Knight returned home and started a new band called Pax. A DJ friend introduced him to The Electric Flag's Barry Goldberg, who convinced Knight to bring the band to Chicago to record some demos. Encouraged by what he heard, Goldberg invited Pax to L.A. to shop for a record deal. But when the band arrived, they found that Goldberg had gone off to rehab for his heroin addiction. The band secured an agent, and played covers gigs in hotel lounges across the southwest.

An opportunity arose when Knight saw a club marquee advertising a show by Delaney & Bonnie. Knight knew Bonnie Lynn O'Farrell when she was a backing singer for Ike & Tina Turner, back in St. Louis before she married Delaney Bramlett. The couple had lost their band when Eric Clapton - who'd toured Europe with them - hired their rhythm section to become Derek and The Dominos. Knight was hired as guitarist, Pax broke up, and he became embroiled in the soap opera that was the Bramlett's relationship until they divorced and the band broke up in 1972. When not playing with Delaney & Bonnie, Knight did sessions for artists like Peter Kaukonen, Chi Coltrane, Marty Balin and Jim Rose. At night, Knight jammed at the infamous Corral club in Topanga, CA, where he met Randy California.

In a 2014 interview with writer Randy Patterson of the Boomer City website, Knight remembered:

I met Randy California and Ed Cassidy from Spirit in those days. The music community back in the late-'60s/early-70s was a beautiful thing. People from all different kinds of bands could get together and play and jam; get kinda stoned, high, trip out and all that kind of stuff. But it was really a great time! It was through us playing together with Randy California and Ed Cassidy, the same thing happened. After we played a couple of times, Randy said, 'I want you to join my band. We've got some gigs that we're gonna do as Spirit, but I'm also working on my first solo album called *Kapt. Kopter.*' I got to record tracks with him on that.

Knight spent more than a decade playing with Randy in various Spirit lineups, starting with his solo *Kapt. Kopter and The (Fabulous) Twirly Birds* album, *Euro-American*, and appearing on live recordings like *Live At La Paloma*, *Two Sides Of A Rainbow* and *Live At Rockpalast 1978*. After leaving the Spirit fold, Knight returned to his roots, forming The Blowin' Smoke Revue - an old-school R&B band performing covers, who have been entertaining Southern California audiences for over 20 years. More recently, Knight put together a side project called Sky King: a psychedelic-rock band playing original material.

Approaching his 78th birthday, Larry Knight continues in the Ed Cassidy tradition of playing until they carry you away.

Appendix: Spirit Playlist and Buying Guide
Playlist
In the Reverend's humble opinion, these are the top 20 Spirit songs (and the albums they appear on).:

1. 'I Got A Line On You' (*The Family That Plays Together*)
2. 'Mr. Skin' (*Twelve Dreams Of Dr. Sardonicus*)
3. '1984' (*Spirit of '84/The Thirteenth Dream*)
4. 'Fresh Garbage' (*Spirit*)
5. 'Nature's Way' (*Twelve Dreams Of Dr. Sardonicus*)
6. 'Taurus' (*Spirit*)
7. 'Uncle Jack' (*Spirit*)
8. 'Animal Zoo' (*Twelve Dreams Of Dr. Sardonicus*)
9. 'Dark Eyed Woman' (*Clear*)
10. 'Burning Love' (*Tent Of Miracles*)
11. 'All Along The Watchtower' (*Future Games*)
12. 'Enchanted Forest' (*Rapture In The Chambers*)
13. 'California Blues' (*California Blues*)
14. 'Magic Fairy Princess' (*Son Of Spirit*)
15. 'Dream Within A Dream' (*The Family That Plays Together*)
16. 'Like A Rolling Stone' (*Spirit of '76*)
17. 'Mellow Morning' (*Feedback*)
18. 'Poor Richard' (*The Family That Plays Together*)
19. 'My Road' (*Spirit of '76*)
20. 'My Friend' (*Potato Land*)

Buying Guide
If you're a newcomer to this incredible band and are not sure where to start, the Reverend has rated the best Spirit albums in buying order. Be forewarned, however - once you start collecting Spirit albums, you're gonna want them all!

1. *Twelve Dreams Of Dr. Sardonicus*
2. *The Family That Plays Together*
3. *Live At Rockpalast 1978*
4. *Spirit*
5. *California Blues*
6. *Live From The Time Coast*
7. *Tent Of Miracles*
8. *Rapture In The Chambers*
9. *Son Of Spirit*
10. *Future Games (A Magical-Kahauna Dream)*

Bibliography

Books

Christgau, R., *Christgau's Record Guide: Rock Albums Of The Seventies* (Ticknor & Fields, 1981)

Knight, B. (editor), *Rick Johnson Reader: 'Tin Cans, Squeems & Thudpies'* (Mayfly Productions, 2007)

Marsh, D., Swenson J. (editors), *The New Rolling Stone Record Guide* (Random House, 1983)

Walker, R., *Hot Wacks Book XV: The Last Wacks* (The Hot Wacks Press, 1992)

Liner Notes

California, R., *Spirit, The Family That Plays Together, Clear, Twelve Dreams Of Dr. Sardonicus* (Legacy Recordings, 1996)

Ferguson, J., *Clear* (Legacy Recordings, 1996)

Locke, J., *Feedback* (Collectors Choice Music, 2003)

Robinson, A., *Spirit Of '76* (BGO Records, 2003), *Son Of Spirit/Farther Along* (BGO Records, 2004), *The Thirteenth Dream* (BGO Records, 2005), *Time Circle 1968-1972* (Sony Music, 1991)

Skidmore, M., *Blues From The Soul* (Acadia Records, 2003), *Live From The Time Coast* (Acadia Records, 2004), *Model Shop* OST (Sundazed Records, 2005), *Sea Dream* (Acadia Records, 2004), *Son Of America* (Acadia Records, 2005), *The Original Potato Land* (Retroworld, 2011), *Tent Of Miracles* (Esoteric Recordings, 2020), *Two Sides Of A Rainbow* (Retroworld, 2012)

Periodicals

Bell, M., 'Spirit of California' (*The History Of Rock* magazine, 1983), 'California Dreaming' (*Classic Rock* magazine, June 2014)

Blake, M., '50 Years of Chaos' (*Mojo* magazine, December 2021)

Breznikar, K., 'Spirit Interview with Mark Andes' (*It's Psychedelic Baby* magazine, June 2018)

Ceriotti, B., 'Stack: Some People Dig On Just Being Alive' (*Ugly Things* magazine, Winter 2021)

Fornatale, M., 'The Original Potato Land' CD review (*Shindig! Quarterly* 3, 2011)

Gerber, M., 'Ed Cassidy dies at 89: drummer for band Spirit' (*Los Angeles Times*, 8 December 2012)

Graham, G., 'Jo Jo Gunne Bite Down Hard' album review (*Creem* magazine, June 1973)

Krakow, S., 'Sunrise and Salvation: The Mercury Era Anthology' album review (*Ugly Things* magazine, Spring 2022)

Lester, P., 'Hidden Treasures: Spirit - Future Games' (*The Guardian*, March 2013)

McMullen, P., 'Randy California Obituary' (*Ptolemaic Terrascope*, 1997)

Mills, J., *Feedback* album review (*Shindig!*, July 2008)

Moody, P., *Twelve Dreams of Dr. Sardonicus* album review (*Classic Rock* magazine, April 2022)

Patterson, R., 'Larry Fuzzy Knight Interview' (boomercity.com, 27 July 2014)

Patterson, T., 'The Old Magician: 20 Questions With Nick Lowe' (*Shindig!* magazine, September 2021)

Perrone, P., 'John Locke Obituary' (*The Independent*, August 15th, 2006)

Rosen, S., 'Behind the Curtain' (*Rock Cellar* magazine, January 2018)

Shade, W., 'The Thieving Magpies: Jimmy Page's Dubious Recording Legacy' (*Perfect Sound Forever* website, 2008)

Skidmore, M., 'Spirit: The Best But Most Neglected L.A. Band From the 60's' (*Relix* magazine, March 2001), 'The Family That Played Together' (*Shindig!* magazine, September 2009)

Swanson, D., 'Top 10 Spirit Songs' (*Ultimate Rock*, December 2012)

Vognsen, J., 'Eugene Chadbourne On Country' (*Perfect Sound Forever* website, 2008)

Internet Resources

www.allmusic.com
www.cherryred.co.uk
www.disccogs.com
www.furious.com
www.genius.com
www.independent.co.uk
www.indiegorock.com
www.jambands.com
www.jojogunne.com
www.lostinmusic.org
www.loudersound.com
www.markandesmusic.com
www.music-lawyer.com
www.peel.fandom.com/wiki/Spirit
www.progarchives.com
www.psychedelicbabymag.com
www.randycaliforniaandspirit.com
www.robertchristgau.com
www.rockcellarmagazine.com
www.setlist.fm
www.sundazed.com
www.terrascope.co.uk
www.ultimateclassicrock.com